CULTURE AND RELIGION.

CULTURE AND RELIGION

IN SOME OF THEIR RELATIONS.

BY

J. C. SHAIRP,

PRINCIPAL OF THE UNITED COLLEGE OF ST. SALVATOR AND ST. LEONARD, ST. ANDREWS.

[*Reprinted from the Edinburgh Edition.*]

NEW YORK:
PUBLISHED BY HURD AND HOUGHTON.
Cambridge: Riverside Press.
1872.

RIVERSIDE, CAMBRIDGE:
STEREOTYPED AND PRINTED BY
H. O. HOUGHTON AND COMPANY.

PREFACE.

THIS little book is a small contribution to a great subject. The five Lectures which it contains were delivered, on five successive Saturdays of last Winter Session, to as many of the Students of the United College and others as chose to attend. They were originally written with a view solely to immediate delivery. The publication of them is an afterthought. It is needless to explain my reasons for publishing them, for these could neither increase nor diminish their value, whatever that may be. One object, however, which I hope may be gained by publication is to place them in a permanent form before those for whom they were originally intended. As lectures, meant to be understood on first hearing, they are naturally in a style more popular and diffuse than might have beseemed a regular treatise. They are printed almost as they were spoken, with the exception of the Fifth Lecture, to which some passages have been added.

It need hardly be said that no attempt is here made at systematic, much less at exhaustive, treatment of the subject. To have aimed at this within the space and in the form to which I have restricted myself, would have been impossible. All I have wished to do is to set forth certain views, which seem to me true in themselves, and yet likely to be passed over too lightly, or set aside too summarily, by the intellectual temper of the time. No satisfactory adjustment of the questions here entertained can, I believe, be reached without assigning to the spiritual side of man's being and of truth a prominence and an importance, which do not seem to have entered into the thoughts of some of the ablest advocates of Culture. Indeed, to many, and these not the most foolish of mankind, Culture seems then only to be worthy of serious regard when it ministers to faith, — when it enables men to see spiritual things more truly and deeply. If it obstructs or dims the vision of these things, as sometimes it does, it then ceases to have for them any value.

In handling subjects on which all men have some thoughts, it is impossible exactly to determine where one's own end and those of others begin. Where, however, I have been aware that any thought or expression of thought has been suggested to me by another writer, I have tried to acknowlege it, either by quoting in the text some of the author's words, or by giving a quotation from his works in the Notes. Of the passages printed in the Appendix, some were directly suggestive of the thought in the text, others are merely adduced as confirmations of it. It would have been easy to have increased the number of the Notes, but they were drawn out at a place remote from libraries, and were taken only from those books which happened to be at hand. J. C. Shairp.

September 1, 1870.

CONTENTS.

CULTURE AND RELIGION

LECTURE I.

THE AIM OF CULTURE — ITS RELATION TO RELIGION.

When one is called, following the practice of former Principals, to lecture to the students of this College on some branch of thought or knowledge, and when, with a single restriction, it is left undefined what the subject shall be, the selection might naturally be supposed to give rise to some embarrassment. But two conditions are at hand to restrict and determine the lecturer's choice. One is, that he must choose some subject with which his past studies or experience have made him in some degree familiar; the other is, that the subject should be such as he may reasonably hope will either interest or benefit his hearers, — if possible, do both.

It seemed to me not unfitting that, on this

first occasion of my lecturing to you in a new capacity, I should speak on some subject of wide and general interest, which commands a view, not so much of any one department of study, as of the last and highest ends of all study.

Other opportunities may be given for taking up some one definite subject, historical or other, and dealing with it in detail.

For this year I shall be well content if, without pretending to overtake, much less exhaust, the wide subject which I bring before you, I shall be enabled to offer a few suggestions, which may be of use to some who hear me, on matters which very nearly concern them. The questions I shall have to touch on might easily be made to land us in the most abstract and speculative investigations. It shall, however, be my endeavor, as far as possible, to keep clear of these, and to put what I have to say in a concrete and practical shape. This I shall do both for other reasons, and especially from the conviction that we in Scotland, by getting hold of all subjects by the metaphysical end of them, often contrive to squeeze out of them whatever vital sap they contain.

The question what it is we aim at in mental cultivation, and what relation this latter bears to religion, cannot be said to be out of place here; for in considering these questions we are brought to contemplate steadily what is the end of university life, and in what relation university life stands to the ultimate ends of life taken as a whole. If a University like this exists for any purpose, I suppose it is to promote mental culture, that is, the cultivation not merely of certain technical and professional faculties, but, over and above these, of the whole man. A few years ago there would have been no need to utter a truism like this; but we live at present in a time of intellectual revulsions. What were till lately held to be first principles are now from time to time made the butts for educational reactionists to jeer at. We have lately heard it asserted by men speaking with some authority that universities and all other places of education exist for one purpose only, — to train men for their special crafts or trades. If they do this well, they are useful; if they do not, they are good for nothing. The belief in any ulterior end beyond this is denied and ridiculed. Yet, in spite of the utilitarian logic of Mr. Lowe, and the more humorous banter of our present Lord Rector, I must still believe that, above and beyond special professional training, there is such a thing as mental culture and enlargement, and that this is an excellent gift in itself, apart from any gain it may bring, and that it is one main end of universities to foster the desire and further the attainment of it. The man, I must still hold, is more than his trade. The spirit that is in each man craves other nourishment than the bread he wins.

I do not, in saying this, forget that we have each our special work in the world to do, — as lawyers, physicians, teachers, ministers, and the like, — and that it tasks all our strength and knowledge to do it. All men, or almost all, are bound to throw themselves vigorously into some one of the known professions, and this not for food and raiment only, but as a necessary part of their moral discipline. Few, very few, there are who, even if their circumstances admit it, can dispense with the wholesome yoke of a profession, and yet live to any good purpose. But while fully acknowledging not only the necessity, but the advantage of being harnessed to some regular profession, and that to succeed in this the finest edge of faculty and the most accurate technical training must be sought, I still believe there is something more than this, and greater, which must never be lost sight of, if we desire to become not mere useful machines or instruments, but complete men. The professional man who, over and above his daily duties and business relations, has learned to feel that he has other relations, wider and more permanent, with all his fellow-beings in all ages, — that he is a debtor for all he has and is to a wider circle of things than that he outwardly comes in contact with, — that he is an heir of all the great and good who have lived before him, — is not on that account a worse workman, and is certainly a higher and better man.

It is not, then, a mere dream, but a very real aim, which they propose who urge us to seek "a fuller, more harmonious development of our humanity, greater freedom from narrowness and prejudice, more width of thought, more expansive sympathies, feelings more catholic and humane, a high and unselfish ideal of life." These are the qualities which university training, if it had its perfect work, might be expected to generate and foster. And it does this by bringing young minds, while they are still plastic, into contact with whatever is best in the past history of the race, — with the great deeds, the high thoughts, the beautiful creations which the best men of former times have bequeathed to us. To learn to know and sympathize with these is the work not of one or two years, but of our whole lives. Yet the process may be said to begin here, and in a special way to belong to the university. For here, if anywhere, it is that the avenues are first opened up which lead to the great storehouse of foregone humanities, — here that our apprehension of these things is first awakened. But a small portion of all this richness we can take in during our short university course, — not much, it may be, in a whole life-time. But it is something to have come to know and feel that these things exist, — exist, too, for us, in as far as we can appropriate them, and to have had our thoughts and desires directed thitherward. When the perception of these things and the love of them have been evoked, culture has begun, and the university life is the natural time for it. If this desire does not begin here, it is not often awakened afterwards.

But what do we mean by this fine word

Culture, so much in vogue at present? What the Greeks naturally expressed by their παιδεία, the Romans by their *humanitas*, we less happily try to express by the more artificial word Culture. The use of it in its present sense is, as far as I know, recent in our language, forced upon us, I suppose, by the German talk about "Bildung." And the shifts we have been put to, to render that German word, seem to show that the thing is with us something of an exotic, rather than native to the soil. When applied to the human being, it means, I suppose, the "educing or drawing forth all that is potentially in a man," the training all the energies and capacities of his being to the highest pitch, and directing them to their true ends. The means that it employs to attain these ends are manifold and various, as manifold as are the experiences of life. But one of the most powerful and characteristic instruments of culture is, as I have said, to bring young and plastic minds into contact with all that is best and greatest in the thoughts, the sentiments, the deeds of past generations of men, in order that these may melt into them and mould the character. But culture is not a product of mere study. Learning may be got from books, but not culture. It is a more living process, and requires that the student shall at times close his books, leave his solitary room, and mingle with his fellow-men. He must seek the intercourse of living hearts as well as of dead books, — especially the companionship of those of his own contemporaries whose minds and characters are fitted to instruct, elevate, and sweeten his own. Another thing required is the discipline which must be carried on by each man in himself, the learning of self-control, the forming of habits, the effort to overcome what is evil and to strengthen what is good in his own nature. But to enumerate all the means of culture would be impossible, seeing they are wide as the world, and the process begins with the cradle, and, we may well believe, does not end with the grave. What, then, is the relation in which a university stands to this great life-process? It may be said to be a sort of microcosm, — a small practical abridgment of an unending book, — a compend of the past thought and cultivation of the race, reduced to the shape and dimensions best fitted to be taken in. And this abridgment or summary of the past experience of the race is applied to young minds just at the age which is most susceptible to receive impressions deeply, and retain them permanently.

Every one must observe to what a large extent the advocates of education nowadays, of the lowest as well as of the highest, agree in urging it for the moral fruits it produces. Remove ignorance, say the advocates of primary education, and you put an end to crime. And though we may doubt the necessity of the alleged sequence, we gladly accept their testimony to the moral aim which all education should imply. The Culturists, again — by which term I mean not those who esteem culture, (as what intelligent man does not?) but those, its exclusive advocates, who recommend it as the one panacea for all the ills of humanity, — the Culturists are never done insisting that it is not for its utilitarian results, not for the technical skill and information it implies, nor for the professional success it may secure, that they value culture, but for its effect in elevating the whole man. They tell us that men, in the last resort, are not formed by rules or precepts, no, nor by what are called moral principles, — that men's lives and characters are determined mainly by their ideal, that is, by the thing they lay to heart and live by, often without themselves being aware of it, by that which they in their inmost souls love, desire, aim at, as the best possibility for themselves and others. By the ideal, therefore, that a man loves, and by his persistency in cleaving to it, and working for it, shall you know what he really is. This ideal, whatever it be, seen and embraced, and melting into a man, constitutes his true and essential nature, and reveals itself in all he thinks and does. They tell us, and truly, that it is not the educated and refined only who have their ideal, — that every man, even the most illiterate, has an ideal, whether he knows it or not; that is, every man has something which forms the ruling thought, the main desire, of his life. The beggar in his rags is not without his ideal, though that probably does not go beyond plenty to eat and drink, and a comfortable house to live in. If he be advanced a little above abject want, then perhaps his ideal is to become wealthy, respected of all men for his riches. These, though material aims, are yet none the less ideals to those who entertain them. The Culturists, then, go on to say that, since every man must have his ideal, — material and selfish, or unselfish and spiritual, — it lies mainly with culture to determine whether men shall rest content with grosser aims or raise their thoughts to the higher ideals. These latter, they remind us, are manifold: there is the ideal poetical, the ideal scientific, the ideal political, the ideal philanthropic: and that which of these, or other such like, a man shall set before him must be determined by his inborn bias and temperament, his natural gifts, and his outward circumstances. There are diversities of gifts, and to every man his own gift. The kind and measure of gifts each man has will shape and modify the ideal which is proper to him. And each man's practical wisdom consists in truly discovering the ideal which naturally belongs to himself, and in so dealing with the facts and circumstances in which his lot is cast, as to reconcile by a true adjustment his inward aspiration and his outward surroundings.

If, then, it be true that every man must have an ideal of some sort, and that this, be it base or lofty, rules his whole being, the Culturists tell us that it is the business of culture to waken men to the consciousness of some ideal, and to set before them true and lofty standards; for the young especially to open up, through the manifold obstructions of sense and outward things, avenues by which the soul may catch some glimpse of the true beauty, the real good, "of that light which being compared with the light is found before it, more beautiful than the sun, and above all the orders of the stars."[1]

They further tell us that it is the business of culture not only to set before men the vision, but to impart to them the cunning hand which shall impress on outward things the pattern of the things seen in the mount. This culture does, by training them in the best knowledge of the time, by imbuing them with as much of the sciences and arts as they can take in and use. Without such practical training of the faculties and the hand, a man, however true his ideal, will become a mere dreamer, powerless to effect anything. And life is so complex, the materials we have to deal with so various and intractable, that it needs long and severe discipline of the faculties to give a man the chance of working his way towards his ideal through the numberless hindrances that surround him.

We see, then, that culture, according to the claim put in for it by its most ardent advocates, is said to do two things: first, it sets before a man a high ideal end to aim at,

[1] Note I.

which shall enter into and control his life; secondly, it trains all the faculties, all the inward powers and outward instruments, — hand, eye, ear, — so as to enable him in some measure to realize that ideal end, and overcome the obstructions that lie between him and it. Such is the claim which is put in by the Culturists. And, after what I have said at the commencement, you will believe that I shall not gainsay it. True as far as it goes, it is, however, far enough from being an adequate account of the whole matter.

Before quitting this subject, let me but add one word in defense of those who speak of ideal aims. Very practical or cynical persons are fond of sneering at these. They make merry, as it is easy to do, with those who, in their phrase, keep vaporing about ideals. What have we, or most men, they say, to do with ideals? Let us leave them to the rapt poet, the recluse thinker, the dreaming visionary. It is the actual, the hard facts of life that we have to deal with; to push our way in the world, maintain the struggle for existence, immersed in the tangible and material, hemmed in by, often nigh crushed beneath, imperious circumstances. Enough for us if we can battle through them, without being overpowered. Ideals! let us leave them to those who have wealth and leisure; they are among the luxuries, not the necessities of life. For us we have enough to do to make something of the real.

To make something of the real! Yes, that's it. But how are we to make anything of the actual unless we have some aim to direct our efforts, some clew to guide us through its labyrinths? And this aim, this clew, is just what is meant by the Ideal. You may dislike the word and reject it, but the thing you cannot get rid of, if you would live any life above that of brutes. An aim, an ideal of some sort, be it material or spiritual, you must have, if you have reason, and look before and after. True, no man's life can be wholly occupied with the ideal, not even the poet's or the philosopher's. Each man must acquaint himself with numberless details; must learn the stuff that the world is made of, and how to deal with it. Even Phidias and Michael Angelo must study the nature of the rough block they have to hew. Not even the most ethereal being can live wholly upon sunbeams, and most lives are far enough removed from the sunbeams. Yet sunshine, light, is necessary for every man. And though most are immersed in business, or battling all life through with tough conditions, yet, if we are not to sink into mere selfish animality, we must needs have some master light to guide us; "something that may dwell upon the heart, though it be not named upon the tongue." For if there be sometimes a danger lest the young enthusiast, through too great devotion to an abstract ideal, should essay the impossible, and break himself against the walls of destiny that hem him in, far more common is it for men to be so crushed under manhood's burdens, that they abandon all the high aims of their youth, and submit to be driven like gin-horses —

> "Round the daily scene
> Of sad subjection, and of sick routine."

The Culturists, then, speak truly when they tell us that every man must have some ideal, and that it is all-important that, while the mind is plastic, each should form some high aim which is true to his own nature, and true to the truth of things. It has been well said that youth is the season when men are engaged in forming their ideals. In mature age they are engaged in trying to impress them on the actual world. And culture professes to effect that men shall fix their aims high and true, and be equipped with the knowledge, skill, aptitudes, required for carrying them out successfully.

But the question now occurs, which has probably suggested itself ere now to some who hear me, What does religion say to all this? We had thought it had been religion which set forth the ends of life, and supplied the motives and the power for striving towards them. But now it seems that there is some rival power, called Culture, which claims for itself these architectonic functions which we had hitherto thought belonged of right to Religion. In the language of Aristotle, which of these two is the architectonic or master-art which prescribes to all the other arts and occupations of life their functions, as the master-builder prescribes their duties to his workmen? Or are Culture and Religion really rival powers? are they to be regarded as in any way antagonistic to each other? And if not, what are their mutual relations? in what way do they meet and act on each other?

This is the question with which I shall have to deal more or less, now leaving it, now returning to it, throughout these Lectures.

One thing is obvious, that, however much the end of life, as laid down by religion, may diverge from the view taken by culture, yet religion will have nothing to say against the assertion that life must be ruled by an aim which shall be ideal. For what can be more ideal than that which religion sets before us? "Seek ye first the kingdom of God." "Be ye perfect, even as your Father in heaven is perfect."

Let this, then, be clearly understood, that whether we look at life from the side of Culture or from that of Religion, in either case we must be guided by an ideal light, which is, indeed, the only real and powerful guidance.

Now as to the relation in which these two stand to each other: —

Culture proposes as its end the carrying of man's nature to its highest perfection, the developing to the full all the capacities of our humanity. If, then, in this view, humanity be contemplated in its totality, and not in some partial side of it, Culture must aim at developing our humanity in its Godward aspect, as well as its mundane aspect. And it must not only recognize the religious side of humanity, but if it tries to assign the due place to each capacity, and assign to all the capacities their mutual relations, it must concede to the Godward capacities that paramount and dominating place which rightfully belongs to them, if they are recognized at all. That is, Culture must embrace Religion, and end in it.

Again, to start from the side or point of view of religion: — The ground of all religion, that which makes it possible, is the relation in which the human soul stands to God. This relation is the root one, and determines what a man really is. As à Kempis says, "What thou art in the sight of God, that thou truly art." The practical recognition of this relation as the deepest, most vital, most permanent one, as that one which embraces and regulates all others, this is religion. And each man is religious just in proportion as he does practically so recognize this bond, which binds him to his Maker.

If, then, religion be this, it must embrace culture: first, because it is itself the culture of the highest capacity of our being; and secondly, because, if not partial and blind, it must acknowledge all the other capacities of man's nature as gifts which God has given, and given that man may cultivate them to the utmost, and elevate them by connecting them with the thought of the Giver, and the purpose for which He gave them.

We see, then, that religion, when it has its perfect work, must lead on to culture. If this view be true, culture and religion are not, when rightly regarded, two opposite powers, but they are as it were one line with two opposite poles. Start from the manward pole, and go along the line honestly and thoroughly, and you land in the divine one. Start from the divine pole, and carry out all that it implies, and you land in the manward pole, or the perfection of humanity. Ideally considered, then, culture must culminate in religion, and religion must expand into culture. So it ought to be, — so, we sometimes imagine, it might be. But it requires little knowledge of history, and a very small observation of men, to convince us that so it has not been in the past, so it is not now. Goethe, the high-priest of culture, loathes Luther, the preacher of righteousness. The earnestness and fervor of the one disturb and offend the calm serenity which the other loves. And Luther, likely enough, had he seen Goethe, would have done him but scant justice.

Mr. Arnold figures to himself Virgil and Shakespeare accompanying the Puritan Pilgrim Fathers on their voyage to America, and asks if the two poets would not have found the company of such men intolerable. If, however, the two poets instead of the Puritan exiles had been thrown into the society of St. Paul and St. John, would they have found their society much more to their mind? These sharp contrasts suggest some questions not easy to answer. It is no use smoothing them over by commonplaces about the one-sidedness of all men, and the limitations of our nature. When, however, we think over it, we can see some reasons which make the combination of the two things difficult, so difficult that it is only in a few, and these rarely gifted natures, that they have both coexisted in any high degree. Take the case of a man who has not had a religious home and childhood, but has begun with culture. It is easy to see that such a one, when from his scientific investigations and philosophical reasonings, or æsthetic ideals, he turns his thoughts for the first time towards religious truth, will come in contact with an order of things that is alien to the ways of thought and repugnant to the modes of feeling engendered in him by culture. The practical thought of God is something so different from the apprehension of any truth of science or philosophy, and puts the mind into such a different posture from any to which these have accustomed it, that the mere man of culture will feel that for such contemplation he either requires new faculties, or must make a new use of the old, and likely enough he will give it up in despair. Again, the account which Christianity gives of human nature, even if we avoid all exaggeration, is not one that readily falls in with the habits either of the scientific or of the poetic mind. The mystery of evil, as its working is described in the Epistle to the Romans, and man's need of redemption, his helplessness until succored by a strength higher than his own: these are truths that do not easily find a place in any system of ordered evolution such as science delights to trace, — rather they are yawning gaps that come in to baffle and perplex all the scientific methods. Nor are they less alien to imaginations that have been fed on the great poetic creations, for these lend themselves readily to the pantheistic idea of evil as a necessary step on the road to good, rather than to the Christian view of sin. In short, the transition from the objects on which culture dwells to those on which religion dwells is the passage from a region in which human thought, human effort, human self-development, are paramount, to a region in which man's own powers are entirely subordinate, in which recipiency, not self-activity, is the primary law of life, and in which the chief worker is not man, but God.

To put the matter forcibly, let me quote the words of a venerable writer still living:[1] "It is impossible," he says, "to look into the Bible with the most ordinary attention without feeling that we have got into a moral atmosphere quite different from that which we breathe in the world, and in the world's literature. In the Bible God is presented as doing everything, and as being the cause and end of everything; and man appears only as he stands related to God, either as a revolted creature or as the subject of Divine grace. Whereas in the world, and in the books which contain the history of the world, according to its own judgment, man appears to do everything, and there is as little reference to God as if there were no such Being in the universe."

[1] See Note II.

These words point to a great but real opposition, to a vast hiatus not to be gainsaid or passed by, — the difference between the point of view of the Bible and of ordinary literature, — the opposed aspects that life wears, according as we accept the religious interpretation of the world or the secular interpretation of it. No doubt it is the great end of Christianity to heal this long-standing discord, to do away the ancient opposition between things divine and things human, to reconcile all true human learning, not less than human hearts, to God. That in every age Christianity has done so in some measure, history is the witness. That it has yet much to do, vast tracts of thought to reclaim and spiritualize, before the reconciliation is complete, if it is ever to be complete, — this is but too apparent.

It may help to make the whole matter clearer, if, before concluding, we cast our eye backward to the sources whence first issued these two great streams of tendency that long since, more or less combined, and now compose the main current of civilization.

Of culture in its intellectual side, of those mental gifts which have educated the civilized world, and moulded thought to what it is, Greece, you all know, is the birth-land. It was there that these gifts sprang to light, and were matured before they were spread abroad and became the inheritance of the nations. The first father, the Apostle of civilization, as he has been called, was Homer. For several centuries the poems of the old minstrel floated about orally, intrusted only to men's memories. But when the Athenian prince gathered together his scattered fragments, and reduced them to writing, "the vagrant ballad-singer" was, as it were, enthroned as the king of minstrelsy, and "invested with the office of forming the young mind of Greece to noble thoughts and bold deeds."[1] Henceforth to be read in Homer became the first requirement of an educated gentleman. And as time went on there followed in due succession all the order of the poets. Didactic, lyric, tragic, comic poetry, each of these in Greece first came to light, and there, too, found its consummate form. Hesiod, Pindar, Æschylus, Sophocles, Aristophanes, — these followed in the train of Homer, and, though subordinate to him, became likewise the teachers of the Greek

[1] Note III.

youth. On poetry followed history, — with Herodotus for the father of pictorial, Thucydides of philosophic, history. And as history came from the consciousness of political life, so also did oratory, which was one of its younger products.

And when all these intellectual forms had nearly completed themselves, last of all, as the maturest creation of Hellenic mind, came philosophy, — philosophy with its countless names and variety of phases, but with Socrates, Plato, and Aristotle standing in the forefront, for all time "the masters of those who know."

No one who looks back on that marvelous fertility, that exhaustless variety of the rarest gifts of thought, the product of so small a land and so few centuries, the wonder of which only increases the more we contemplate it, can believe that it was intended to begin and end in the land which gave it birth, — that these words of sayers and thinkers had fulfilled the end they were designed for when they had delighted or instructed only the men who first heard them. No; the idea must force itself on every one who really reflects on it that this inexhaustible richness was given to Athens, that she might be the intellectual mother of the world, — that her thoughts might be a possession for all ages.

Just as we see that the long geological epoch, which stored up the vast coal measures, was evidently preparing those material resources which were not only to minister to the physical comfort, but to create the physical civilization of great nations yet to be, even so this exuberance of intellectual wealth seems, in the design of the world, to have been so marvelously matured in Greece, that it might be as a treasure-house from which not so much the Greeks themselves as all future generations might be schooled, elevated, and refined.

With regard to the action of Hellenic thought, however, two remarks are to be made. The first is, it was not so much immediately and directly, as by creating Latin literature and reaching modern thought through the medium of the Latin language, that Greece has propelled European civilization. It was not till the revival of letters in the fifteenth century that Greek thought came face to face with the modern world, and infused itself directly into western culture. Of course it is an old remark that in literature Rome produced little original, and mainly imitated Greece. But when we look at it, there is more in this than at first appears. It is, as has been well said, "a proof of the sort of instinct which has guided the course of civilization. The world was to have certain intellectual teachers, and no others. Homer and Aristotle, with the poets and philosophers who circle round them, were to be the schoolmasters of all generations; and therefore the Latins, falling into the law on which the world's education was to be carried on, so added to the classical library as not to reverse or interfere with what had been already determined."

The second remark I would offer is, that whatever else Greece has given to the world, however much she may have educated men to clear and subtle thought, and to the delicate sense of beauty, and to the highest forms of abstract thinking, it is not Greece that has awakened and satisfied the religious longings of humanity. Indeed, it is a very noteworthy fact, that before Hellenic thought became cosmopolitan, it dropped the native ethnic religion, and left it behind in the place of its birth as a residuum that could not live elsewhere. What was purely intellectual, that was catholic and fitted for all time; what was religious, that was local, temporary, and doomed to perish. Connected with this fact is the divorce in Greece between religion and morality, in all but a very few of her highest minds. Indeed, it is observable how, as the moral sense of the Hellenic race grew deeper and wider, the original religion of Homer fell off from it as felt to be inadequate.

Greece, then, was the source of intellectual culture; but we must look to a remoter and more eastern land to find the original source of religious knowledge. "Jerusalem," as has been said, "is the fountain-head of religious knowledge to the world, as Athens is of secular." The ancient world contained these two, and only these two, centres of illumination, separate and independent, to which the modern world is indebted for the highest gifts of human learning and the life-giving powers of divine grace. Greece, while it enlightened and delighted the intellect, left the conscience and spirit of man unsatisfied. To meet the wants of these, to reach man in the deepest seats of his being, it required something more inward, more penetrating, more vital. It required the simple yet profound truths of that revelation which began and was perfected in Judæa.

With regard to the teaching of that revelation, I will note but two things. One is, that to the Hebrew mind the thought of morality and the thought of God were never separate, but were ever essentially at one. That word belongs to the oldest record of the Hebrew race, "Shall not the Judge of all the earth do right?" And this interpenetration of morality and religion, which pervades the teachings alike of lawgiver, psalmist, and prophet, finds its perfect consummation in Him in whom the revelation culminated and closed. The other thing I would remark is the striking fact that it was from amidst a people hitherto the most isolated and exclusive of all known peoples, — a nation shut off from all the world by the most narrow restrictions and prejudices, — that there arose, in all the force of living conviction, a faith the most unrestricted, the most expansive, and all-embracing which the world had hitherto known or ever can know.

When we think on these two separate centres of illumination, — "the grace stored in Jerusalem, and the gifts which radiate from Athens," — the thought cannot but occur, How do these two stand related to each other? In that expression, "when the fullness of the time was come," no thoughtful student of history can fail to recognize, along with the preparations that had gone on in Judæa, some reference to the work which Greece and Rome had done on the earth. You remember that superscription which was written in letters of Greek, and Latin, and Hebrew. That superscription seems to symbolize the confluence of powers which thenceforward were to rule the minds of men. That central grace and truth which came by Jesus Christ was to go forth into the world embodied in the language which had been long since fashioned by Homer and Plato, and that Hellenic tongue in its last decadence was to be made "the vehicle of higher truths and a holier inspiration than had ever haunted the dreams of bard or sage in old Achaia." And not less, in order that the glad tidings might spread abroad, was needed the political action of Rome. The world had first to be leveled down into one vast empire, and the stern legionaries, — "those massive hammers of the whole earth," — as they paved the great highways from the Euphrates to the Pillars of Hercules, were, though they knew it not, fulfillers of Hebrew prophecy, and preparing the way of the Lord and making straight in the desert a highway for our God. So it was that Judæa, Greece, and Rome combined to make possible the new creation. Not in Judæa alone, but in the other two countries also, there had been going on, as has been well said, "a moral and spiritual expansion, which rendered the world more capable of apprehending the Gospel than it would have been in any earlier age." If there is anything providential at all in human history, this convergence of influences to bring about "the fullness of the time" must be regarded as such.

The agencies which in those past ages combined to form Christendom have their points of contact and cohesion; they have also their points of divergence and repulsion. During some epochs the harmony of their working has been conspicuous; in other epochs, for a time at least, they have seemed rather to be divergent. But however much, in certain turning-points of human thought, these great influences, or their modern representatives, may seem for a time to collide, and though in the collision many individuals may suffer grievous loss, one cannot but believe that out of the conflict of earnest though one-sided convictions, there will at length arise, as there has done in past ages, a revivified faith, a harmony of elements, more simple, more all-embracing, more spiritual than any that has yet been.

LECTURE II.

THE SCIENTIFIC THEORY OF CULTURE.

I ENDEAVORED in my last lecture to bring before you the meaning of culture as understood by those who most warmly advocate it, the ends it proposes, the means by which it seeks those ends. There was less need to dwell at length on the nature of religion, as this, we may assume, is more commonly understood. We saw that these two, though distinct in their nature, and starting from different points of view, are not really opposed. For culture, if thoroughly and consistently carried out, must lead on to religion, that is, to the cultivation of the spiritual and heavenward capacities of our nature. And religion, if truthful and wise, must expand into culture, must urge men who are under its power to make the most of all their capacities, not only for the worth of these capacities in themselves, but because they are gifts of God, and given for this purpose, that we may carefully cultivate them. And no doubt culture, pursued under such a feeling, would acquire a new worth; it would be purified from egotism and unhealthy self-consciousness, would be informed by a more chastened, reverential spirit, which would add to it a new excellence. If we could but attain and keep the highest and truest point of view, and regard "humanity as seen in the light of God," all good gifts of nature and of art would fall into their right place, for they would assume in our thoughts that place which they have in the creative thought of the Giver.

So it is in truth; but so we saw it has not been in fact. We saw that often it has happened that culture has taken account of all man's capacities but the highest, and so has become Godless; on the other hand, that often sincere religion has thought it was honoring things spiritual by depreciating the cultivation of the lower but yet essential capacities of man, and so has narrowed itself, and cut itself off from reality.

I then glanced at the two historical centres of illumination, from the one of which the world had received its spiritual, from the other its intellectual light, and I noted how these two had providentially combined to bring in the new creation of Christianity. At the close I was led to remark that while these two mighty influences had combined, and doubtless were intended to combine, to bless mankind, one could not but perceive that as they contain elements which draw to each other and tend to coalesce, so they contain other elements which may tend, and at certain epochs have tended to divergence, or even to collision.

Such an epoch was that wakening of the European mind in the fifteenth and sixteenth centuries, known as the revival of letters. When the fall of Constantinople had sent crowds of Greek exiles westward, bearing with them their Greek learning into Italy, — when the printing press, newly invented, was pouring forth year by year fresh editions of Greek and Latin classics, — when the discovery of another hemisphere had opened a boundless horizon for enterprise and civilization, — the minds of men, long hide-bound in scholastic logic and theology, sprang forward, as from a musty prison-house, into a fresh world of light. In Florence, then the fountain-head of the revived learning, the recoil from the outworn paths drove many minds not only from scholasticism, but even from Christianity. They fancied they could find something better, wider, more human in a semi-pagan philosophy. Intoxicated, as was not unnatural, by the fascinations of the new learning, they imagined that in it alone they had found an all-sufficient portion.

Again, about the beginning of last century, the same tendency to discard religion, at least revealed religion, and to make the products of human learning take its place, set in, though in another form. After the religious wars, as they are called, of the seventeenth century had been fought out; after the strong Puritan movement had spent itself, there came on a period of active philosophizing, but of philosophy unaccompanied by spiritual insight. As you read the works of Bishop Butler, you seem to hear the voice of a great and earnest thinker crying in the wilderness, and pleading with a suffering generation to believe that there is a deeper moral tendency in things than at first sight appears. It was a sifting, active-minded age, analyzing all things and believing in nothing which it could not analyze ; an age wholly over-mastered by the understanding, judging according to sense.

So it was for the greater part of last century. But Germany before the French Revolution, and our own country after it, startled by the conclusions to which the Sense-philosophy had led in all departments of life, and the devastation it had made among all man's chiefest instincts and most cherished faiths, awoke to think over again those great problems which the past age had settled and dismissed so complacently. The human mind plunged down as it were to a deeper layer of thought and feeling than that which had satisfied the age of the Aufklärung, as it is called. The philosophy of Voltaire and Hume could hold it no longer. This recoil manifested itself in Germany by the rise of the Kantian philosophy and the succession of great idealistic systems that followed it. In this country it was seen in here and there an attempt at a deeper metaphysic than that of Locke and Hume, but much more in the increased depth and compass of the poetry and literature of the first fifty years of this century. Everywhere that literature is pervaded by greater reach of thought, increased tenderness, more reverence, finer aspiration. In most of its greater poets there is something of the

> "Tendebantque manus ripæ ulterioris amore," —

the stretching forth the hands in yearning for a farther shore. It is clear that when culture is in such a phase, it more readily allies itself with religion than when it is sense-bound, unenthusiastic, and analytic mainly of the more obvious phenomena.

The years about 1840 may be taken as the time when the spiritual flood-tide had reached the full. It is always very difficult to estimate the age in which you are living, yet I think we seem to have come in during the last twenty years for the ebb of that spiritual wave. Wordsworth, in his day, complained that —

> "Plain living and high thinking are no more."

Of our day it may be truly said that high living and plain thinking are the all in all. In an age of great material prosperity like the present, when the comforts and conveniences of physical life have greatly increased, and science is every day increasing them, this world is apt to seem in itself a "satisfying abode," quite irrespective of any hope beyond. The spread of knowledge is doing so much to remove many of the surface ills of life, that vague and exaggerated hopes are apt to be fostered of what it may yet do for the healing of the deepest disorders. To minds that have got themselves intoxicated with notions of material progress, this world, as I have said, is apt to seem enough, and man to appear a satisfying object to himself quite apart from God.

This tendency, I think, manifests itself, as in other things, so also in some theories of culture which have lately been propounded. In these we see the attempt made either to substitute for religion the last and highest results of knowledge and culture, or to bring religion down from its supremacy, and give the highest place to culture.

The first view which I shall bring before you, and which will occupy the rest of our time to-day, is that which is taken by the advocates of a rigorous and exclusively scientific culture, by those who would make the scientific method our only guide in life, not merely in things belonging to the physical order, but not less in the highest concerns of the human spirit. As tendencies are best seen in an extreme instance, I shall take as the sample of this tendency an inaugural lecture delivered about two years ago by Professor Huxley, at the South London Working Men's College, of which he was then President. It is entitled "A Liberal Education, and where to find it." There is this advantage in taking the instance I have chosen, that it presents in a strong and easily understood form a way of thinking which in less aggravated degree pervades very widely the intellectual atmosphere of our time.

Mr. Huxley lays down as his first principle, that education, in its largest and highest sense, — the education not merely of schools and colleges, but that education which the human spirit is receiving uninterruptedly from birth till death, — that this process consists solely in learning the laws of nature, and training one's self to obey them. And within the laws of nature which we have to learn he includes not only the physical laws, but also those moral laws which govern man and his ways. We must set ourselves therefore to acquire a knowledge not only of the laws that regulate matter, but also of the moral laws of the universe. These moral laws Mr. Huxley holds to be as rigid and self-exacting as the physical laws appear to be. This view of the condition of our existence here, and of the part which man bears in it, Mr. Huxley sets forth in a startling, not to say daring, figure. "Suppose it were perfectly certain," he says, "that the life and fortune of every one of us would, one day or another, depend upon his winning or losing a game of chess, don't you think that we should all consider it to be a primary duty to learn at least the name and moves of the pieces; to have a notion of a gambit, and a keen eye for all the means of giving and getting out of a check? Do you not think we should look with a disapprobation amounting to scorn upon the father who allowed his son, or the state which allowed its members, to grow up without knowing a pawn from a knight?

"Yet it is a very plain and elementary truth that the life, the fortune, and the happiness of every one of us, and, more or less, of those connected with us, do depend on our knowing something of the rules of a game infinitely more difficult and complicated than chess. It is a game which has been played for untold ages, every man and woman of us being one of the two players in a game of his or her own. The chess-board is the world, the pieces are the phenomena of the universe, the rules of the game are what we call the laws of nature. The player on the other side is hidden from us. We know that his play is always fair, just, and patient. But we know, to our cost, that he never overlooks a mistake or makes the smallest allowance for ignorance. To the man who plays well the highest stakes are paid with that overflowing generosity with which the strong shows delight in strength. And one who plays ill is checkmated, without haste, but without remorse. My metaphor," Professor Huxley proceeds, "will remind some of you of the famous picture in which Retzsch has depicted Satan playing chess with a man for his soul. Substitute for the mocking fiend in that picture a calm, strong angel, who is playing for love, as we say, and would rather lose than win, and I should accept it as an image of human life. Well, what I mean by education is learning the rules of this mighty game. In other words, education is the instruction of the intellect in the laws of nature, under which name

I include not merely things and their forces, but men and their ways, and the fashioning of the affections and the will into an earnest and loving desire to move in harmony with these laws. For me education means neither more nor less than this."

Now, painful as such a view of life must be to those who have been trained in a devouter school, it is well that we should look at it steadily, and try to understand and interpret it fairly. For it is a strong exposition of a way of thinking very prevalent at the present time, which contains a peculiar fascination for many minds which, impatient of mystery, long, before all things, to attain and hold a clearly cut and systematic view. Definiteness is with them the test of truth, and this theory is so definite. However, let us first get Professor Huxley's whole statement. After setting it forth in that startling metaphor, he goes on to remark that nature begins the education of her children before the schools do, and continues it after. She takes men in hand as soon as they are born, and begins to educate them. It is a rough kind of education, one in which "ignorance is treated like willful disobedience, incapacity is punished as a crime. It is not even a word and a blow, but the blow first without the word. It is left to you to find out why your ears are boxed." Now here man comes in, and takes up the process which nature has begun. And the aim of the artificial education which he gives in schools and colleges is, or ought to be, to make good the defects in nature's methods, to prepare the child to receive nature's teaching, and to perfect it. All artificial education should be an anticipation of nature's education; and a liberal education is an artificial education, one which has prepared a man, not only to escape nature's cuffs and blows, but to seize the rewards which she scatters no less lavishly.

Then Mr. Huxley gives us the following picture of what he conceives an educated man to be, as the result of a truly liberal education: —

"That man, I think, has had a liberal education who has been so trained in youth that his body is the ready servant of his will, and does with ease and pleasure all the work that, as a mechanism, it is capable of; whose intellect is a clear, cold, logic engine, with all its parts of equal strength, and in smooth working order; ready, like a steam-engine, to be turned to any kind of work, and spin the gossamers as well as forge the anchors of the mind; whose mind is stored with a knowledge of the great and fundamental truths of nature, and of the laws of her operations; one who, no stunted ascetic, is full of life and fire, but whose passions are trained to come to heel by a vigorous will, the servant of a tender conscience; who has learned to love all beauty, whether of nature or art, to hate all vileness, and to respect others as himself."

This, whatever defects it may have, must be allowed to be, in many ways, a high ideal of education. Though it gives the chief promise to physical nature, and the scientific knowledge of it, yet the moral side of man is by no means forgotten. Mr. Huxley's ideally-educated man is to have his passions trained to obey a strong will; this will is to be the servant of a tender conscience; he is to love beauty, to hate vileness, to respect others as himself. I would have you mark these things, both that we may do full justice to this view, and that we may the better understand the radical defect under which this whole theory of the world labors.

The first remark I would make is, that it takes for granted and founds on that theory of knowledge which is known as pure and exclusive phenomenalism. Phenomenalism, you know, is that philosophy which holds that all existences, all possible objects of thought, are of two kinds only, external and internal phenomena; or sensuous objects, such as color, shape, hardness, or groups of these, and the unsensuous ideas we have of sensuous objects. If, however, we add that there is a third kind of existence, or object of thought, not included in either of those classes already named, but distinct and different from these, namely, "the unsensuous percipients, or spirits or egos, which we are each of us conscious that we ourselves are," then we turn the flank of this philosophy; the inadequacy of the theory on which Mr. Huxley's view is based becomes at once apparent. But into this matter, pertinent though it is to our discussion, I will not enter. For, as I have already said, I wish in these lectures to enter as little as possible into questions purely metaphysical.[1]

The second remark I would make is, that this so-called scientific theory of life implies

[1] Note IV.

that, though probably there is some power behind the phenomena, we have no means of ascertaining what mind and character it is of what purpose it has in creating and upholding this universe, if indeed it did create and does uphold it. I think I am not misinterpreting Professor Huxley when I assume that he holds that our only means of conjecturing what is the mind of the great chess-player he figures, lie in the scientific investigation of the facts of the world. Now, Hume long ago observed that if we judge merely by the facts of the world, we cannot infer any fixed character in the Divine Being; but, if we infer character at all, it must be a two-sided, inconsistent character, partly benevolent, partly the contrary.

As it has been well expressed, the theory comes to this, that "we, as intelligent, thinking beings, find ourselves in a universe which meets us at all points with fixed laws, which encompass us about externally, and rule us also within; fixed laws in the region of matter, fixed laws in the region of mind; that, therefore, knowledge for us is knowledge of laws, and can be nothing more; and that wisdom in us is simply the skill to turn the knowledge of these laws to the best account, conforming ourselves to them, and availing ourselves of them to appropriate to ourselves all the good they bring within our reach." A dreary prospect it would be if science really shut us up to this. Well may it be said that "men of keener hearts would be overpowered with despondency, and would even loathe existence, did they suppose themselves under the mere operation of fixed laws, powerless to excite the pity or the attention of Him who appointed them." If, however, truth compelled us to admit it, we might try to bear up under it as best we could. But is it truth, or only a one-sided philosophy, that shuts us into this corner? That it is not truth, the following considerations will, I hope, help to convince us.

Observe, then, that while Professor Huxley's ideal man is to respect others as himself, we are not told how or whence this most desirable habit of mind is to be engendered. As a man of science, Professor Huxley is bound to take note of facts before all things, and to pass over none. In this very lecture he declares himself to have the greatest respect for all facts. Now, if there is one fact about human nature more certain than another, it is that men do not naturally respect the welfare of others, — rather that "all men seek their own," not the things which belong to their fellow-men. It takes much moral discipline to overcome this inborn propensity. Experience has, I believe, proved that it cannot be overcome except by a man being taken out of self as his centre, and finding a new centre out from and above himself, on which he can rest, to which all men stand equally related, on which all can rest even as he. But Professor Huxley's theory supplies no such centre. If life were really such a game as he describes, — if men were once convinced that they had to do with only such a hidden chess-player as he pictures, would they not more than ever be driven inward, would not the natural selfishness be tenfold more concentrated and intensified?

To bring a man near the Christian requirement, to love his neighbor as himself, takes the whole weight of Christian motive; nothing less will avail. Assuredly the consideration of the evil consequences that will come to one's self from an opposite line of conduct, — which seems to be the moral theory recognized in this lecture, — will be powerless to do so. We conclude, therefore, and say that the merely scientific view of Culture will not work for want of a lever. It postulates as one of its ingredients respect for others, yet it provides no means for securing the presence of that ingredient.

Again, another element which it postulates is "a vigorous will, the servant of a tender conscience." Now, a tender conscience, a true and quick sense of right, and the habit of obeying it, are not born in men ready-made and full formed. The elements, indeed, of such a conscience lie in all men, but it requires long, careful, and delicate training to bring them to maturity. Mr. Huxley has not told us what resources his theory supplies for maturing such a conscience. If the world were to come to recognize no other moral sanctions than those which utilitarianism insists on, would its morality continue to be even as high as it now is? I think not. Certainly if men were once convinced that they were placed in such a world as Professor Huxley pictures, — that their relations to its Ruler were such as he describes, — a tender conscience would be the last thing which would be engendered by such a conviction. We know how children grow up who are reared in homes where no kindness is, but where the only rule is a word and a blow. The rule of terror, whether by parents or teachers, does not generally result in a tender conscience, but in hardness, suspiciousness, deception. If the universe were believed to be such a home or school on a larger scale, would the result be different? In other words, would a tender conscience be produced by the mere study of the laws of the game?

But again, let us suppose such a conscience to exist, and to be active in a man. Such a one, in proportion as the moral nature in him was true and strong, would desire the right to prevail in his own life and in the life of all men, — the desire of his heart would be to see the reign of righteousness established. How would such a man feel, what would be his position, confronted with the Hidden Player, who moves the phenomena of the universe, in whose hand he knows his own life and the life of all men are? — the man loving right, and desiring to see it prevail, the Great Automaton with whom he has to do, being either regardless of it, or affording to men no evidence that he does regard it.

In such circumstances would not the tender conscience be a most inconvenient possession? Would not he who had it feel that it put him out of harmony with the universe in which he was placed? For his best endeavors would find no sympathy, no response in the purpose of Him who rules the universe. What would remain to such a man except either to rid himself of this sensitive conscience, which he found to be no help but rather a hindrance to successful playing of the game, or to desire to get out of a world, as soon as may be, in which the best part of his nature found itself strange and out of place.

But again, this leads me to observe that Professor Huxley's theory either goes too far or not far enough, to be consistent. He ought either to have excluded moral considerations entirely, and to have confined his view wholly to visible and tangible issues; or, if he once introduced moral elements into his theory, these necessitated his going further. Indeed, if we once bring in the higher or spiritual issues of the game, these put an end to the aptness of the similitude, and destroy all its illustrative force. For consider. Each move in the game, that is, each human action, has two sides, — a double aspect; it has its visible and tangible result; it has also its invisible and moral character.[1] And this last, though not recognized by sense, and even when wholly disregarded by men, still exists as really as the seen result. If we regard the moves solely in their first aspect, a man may contrive so to play the game of life as to secure a large amount of visible success, to get for himself most of the good things of this world, health, riches, reputation of a sort, long life, without any very tender conscience. To do this requires only worldly wisdom, only an average stock of market morality. For this kind of success a higher, more sensitive morality is so far from being necessary that it is actually a hindrance. But look at the moves on their spiritual side, weigh success in a moral balance, and our whole estimate is changed. He who is soonest checkmated, he who, judging by what is seen merely, comes by the earliest, most disastrous defeat, may in reality have won the highest moral victory. Such are they who in each age have jeoparded their lives for the truth, those who have been willing to lose life that they might

[1] Note V.

find it, who against the world have stood for right, and in that contest have sacrificed themselves, and by that sacrifice have made all future generations their debtors. They were losers, indeed, of the visible game, but they were winners of the invisible and spiritual one. They had for their reward not what the world calls success, but the sense that they were servants of the truth, doers of the right, and that in doing it they had the approval and sympathy of Him with whom

> "A noble aim,
> Faithfully kept, is as a noble deed,
> In whose pure sight all virtue doth succeed."

This view of things, however, takes into account a fact which Mr. Huxley has failed to recognize, that there is an open path between the soul and God. The thought of this relation, the sense of His approval, forms no part of the success which the mere worldly player aims at. But other men of finer spirit have, in the very crisis of earthly failure, felt the sense of this approval to have been an over-payment for all they suffered.

Indeed, the longer we reflect on the aim which Professor Huxley's theory assigns to human existence, the more will it be seen to contradict, I will not say the best aspirations, but the most indubitable facts of man's higher nature. If life were indeed nothing more than such a game, who would be truly reckoned the most successful players? Not the select spirits of the race, but the men of merely average morality, those whose guide in life was mere prudence, a well-calculated regard to self-interest; while the nobler spirits, those who sought to raise themselves and others to purer heights of being, would find that they were mere irrelevant creatures. All that was best and purest in them would be objectless, an anomaly and disturbance, in such a universe. For it would contain nothing which could so much as warrant their finer perceptions to exist. Or again, look at this other fact, or perhaps it is the same fact put in another light: there is at the core of all men something which the whole world of nature, of science and of art, is inadequate to fill. And this part of man is no mere adjunct of his nature, but his very, most permanent, highest self. What this inmost personality craves is sympathy with something like itself, yet high above it, — a will consubstantial with our better will, yet transcending, supporting, controlling it. This longing is, I believe, latent in all men, though they may not be aware of it. But in the best men it not only exists in latency, but is paramount, — the animating principle of their lives. Of them that ancient word is literally true, "their soul is athirst for God." The desire to have their will conformed to His will, the hope that they shall yet be brought into perfect sympathy with Him, is what in their estimate makes the chief good of existence. They believed that they could know something of the character of God, and that they might reasonably aspire to grow in likeness to that character. This belief has been the root out of which has grown, I will not say all, but certainly much of, the finest flower of morality that has bloomed on earth. It is not easy to believe that what was so true and excellent had its root in a delusion; yet this is the conclusion to which the chess-playing theory, if true, would force us.

But there is a further fact regarding these men which we must not pass over: they have left it on record that their seeking to know God and find rest in Him was not in vain, but that in proportion as they sought in singleness of will to know Him, not with the understanding only, but with their whole spirit, they did really grow in that knowledge. They have told us that, darkly though they here saw, and imperfectly, yet the vision they had was better than anything else they knew of, that compared with it earthly success and merely secular knowledge seemed to them of but little moment. And as to the laws of nature, these, they have told us, had for them a new meaning and a higher value when they saw in them a discipline leading up to the knowledge of Him who ordained them, and as being in their order and marvelous adaptations a reflection of His wisdom and will.

This is the witness they gave of themselves, and the lives they lived and the works they did confirm that witness. Their lives and deeds, making allowance for human infirmity, were in keeping with what they declared respecting themselves. With reason, I think, we may trust them, when they add that the things they did on earth they were enabled to do by a strength which was not of themselves, but which, when they sought it from a source above themselves, they found.

My examination of the theory which has to-day engaged us has led me to observe two things: —

First, That of the moral elements of human nature which that theory postulates, it gives no sufficient account; it provides nothing which shall insure their presence.

Secondly, That it leaves out facts of man's nature which are as certain, though it may be not so apparent, as gravitation, or any other fact which science registers. These facts are indubitable; and the truly scientific spirit would lead man to give heed to them, and ask what they really mean. The spiritual facts of human nature to which I have adverted, no doubt imply, as their support, other facts which are above nature, — an outcoming of the Divine will in a special way, manifesting itself among the phenomena it has made, for the purpose of reaching the human wills which are dependent on it. But this, and all the wonderful economy it implies, I have refrained from speaking of to-day, that I might fix attention all the more clearly on those moral facts which are part of our own experience, but which are apt to be disregarded in comparison with other facts more obvious, but not more real.

In conclusion, let me note a mental bias against which persons, both of scientific and metaphysical turn, do well to be on their guard. Their habits of inquiry sometimes lead them to demand, in proof of things spiritual, a kind of evidence which the subject does not admit, and to be insensible to the kind of evidence which it does admit. Habits of scientific investigation are exceptional, and must always be confined to a few. Christianity is meant for all men. It makes its appeal, not to that in which men differ, but to that which they have in common, — to those primary instincts, sentiments, judgments which belong to all men as men. Therefore it is no unreasonable demand to make, that the man of science, when judging of the things of the spirit, shall leave his solitary eminence, and place himself among the sympathies and needs which he shares with all men, and judge of the claim which religion makes on him, not from the exceptional point of view which he shares only with a few, but from that ground which he occupies in common with his poorest, least scientific brothers.

In asking this we are not asking that he should place his higher faculty in abeyance, and employ a lower in order to weigh and accept religious truth. The logical or scientific faculty, that by which we discern logical, mathematical, or scientific relations, is not the highest exercise of reason. The knowledge of the highest things, those which most deeply concern us, is not attained by mere intellect, but by the harmonious action of understanding, imagination, feeling, conscience, will, — that is, of the whole man. This is reason in its highest exercise, intelligence raised to its highest power; and it is to this exercise of reason we are called in apprehending the things of God.

It is well that we should be convinced, on rational grounds, that science simply as science can never reach God. To him who insists on a purely scientific solution of the problem of man's life and destiny, and who will accept no other, there is no solution; and for this reason: the highest concerns of humanity, the greatest objects with which the soul has to do, cannot even be apprehended by the scientific faculty. If apprehended at all, it must be by the exercise of quite another side of our being than that which science calls into play. "No telescope will enable us to see God. No finest microscope will make Him visible, in the act of working. No chemistry, no study of physical forces, no search after the one primary force, can bring us one 'hand-breadth nearer God.' Science in the abeyance of our spiritual nature attains not to God. No scientific study of the phenomena which imply a reign of law could ever have issued in the discovery of the kingdom of God ; but neither can it issue in any discovery that contradicts that kingdom." These are the words of Dr. M'Leod Campbell, whose writings I have found peculiarly suggestive on the questions I have been discussing.

Therefore it is of no use — indeed, it is a grave error — when those who contend for the religious view of the world attempt to prove to men of science, as if found in science, that which merely scientific faculty will never find there, but which has been brought thither by their faith. Indeed, scientific men, who are also religious, will be the first to acknowledge that their faith in God they did not get from science, but from quite another source ; although this faith, when once possessed, invested with a new meaning, and illumined with a higher light, all that science taught them.

LECTURE III.

THE LITERARY THEORY OF CULTURE.

A TRUE poet and brilliant critic of the present time, admired by all for his fine and cultivated genius, and to me endeared by never-fading memories of early companionship, has identified his name with a very different view of culture from that which I brought before you the last time I addressed you. If Professor Huxley's is the exclusively scientific view of culture, Mr. Arnold's may be called the literary or æsthetic one. In discussing the former theory, I attempted to examine it in the light of facts, and to avoid applying to it any words which its author might disown. For mere appeal to popular prejudice should have no place in discussions about truth, and he who has recourse to that weapon in so far weakens the cause he advocates. If, however, I was constrained to call attention to some not unimportant facts of human nature which that theory fails to account for, this should be regarded not as appeal to unreasoning prejudice, but as a statement of omitted facts. But whatever might be said of Professor Huxley's view, as leaving out of sight the spiritual capacities and needs of man, the same objection cannot equally be urged against Mr. Arnold's theory of culture. He fully recognizes religion as an element, and a very important one, in his theory; only we may see cause to differ from him in the place which he assigns to it. Though I believe Mr. Arnold's theory to be defective when taken as a total philosophy of life, yet so large-minded and generous are the views it exhibits, so high and refined are the motives it urges for self-improvement, that I believe no one can seriously and candidly consider what he says without deriving good from it. As a recent writer has truly said, — "The author of this theory deserves much praise for having brought the subject before men's minds, and forced a little unwilling examination on the 'self-complacent but very uncultured British public.'"

Many who now hear me may have probably read in Mr. Arnold's several works all his pleadings for culture. To these the recapitulation of his views which I shall give may be somewhat tedious, but I hope those who know his writings will bear with me while I briefly go over his views, for the sake of those of my hearers who may be less acquainted with them.

Those who were present at my first lecture may remember that I tried to describe what is meant by culture. That description was not identical with the one I have now to give, but, though different in form, the two will not, I believe, conflict.

In Mr. Arnold's view, the aim of culture is not merely to render an intelligent being more intelligent, to improve our capacities to the uttermost, but, in words which he borrows from Bishop Wilson, "to make reason and the kingdom of God prevail." It is impelled not merely by the scientific desire to see things as they are, but rather by the moral endeavor to know more and more the universal order, which seems intended in the world, that we may conform to it ourselves, and make others conform to it; in short, that we may help to make the will of God prevail in us and around us. In this, he says, is seen the moral, social, beneficent nature of culture, that while it seeks the best knowledge, the highest science that is to be had, it seeks them in order to make them tell on human life and character.

The aim of culture, therefore, is the perfection of our human nature on all its sides, in all its capacities. First, it tries to determine in what this perfection consists, and, in order to solve this question, it consults the manifold human experience that has expressed itself in such diverse ways, throughout science, poetry, philosophy, history, as well as through religion.

And the conclusion which culture reaches is, Mr. Arnold holds, in harmony with the voice of religion. For it places human perfection in an internal condition of soul, in the growth and predominance of our humanity proper, as distinguished from our animality.

Again, it does not rest content with any condition of soul, however excellent, but presses ever onwards to an ampler growth, to a gradual harmonious expansion of those gifts of thought and feeling which make the peculiar dignity, wealth and happiness of human nature. Not a having and resting, but a growing and becoming, is the true character of perfection as culture conceives it.

Again, in virtue of that bond of brotherhood which binds all men to each other, whether they will it or not, this perfection cannot be an isolated individual perfection. Unless the obligation it lays on each man to consider others as well as himself is recognized, the perfection attained must be a stunted, ignoble one, far short of true perfection.

In all these three considerations the aim of culture, Mr. Arnold thinks, coincides with the aim of religion.

First, in that it places perfection not in any external good, but in an internal condition of soul, — "The kingdom of God is within you."

Secondly, in that it sets before men a condition not of having and resting, but of growing and becoming as the true aim, — "Forgetting those things which are behind, and reaching forth unto those things which are before."

Thirdly, in that it holds that a man's perfection cannot be self-contained, but must embrace the good of others equally with his own, and as the very condition of his own, — "Look not every man on his own things, but every man also on the things of others."

These three notes belong alike to the perfection which culture aims at, and to that which religion enjoins.

But there is a fourth note of perfection as conceived by culture, in which, as Mr. Arnold thinks, it transcends the aim of religion. "As an harmonious expansion of ALL the powers which make the beauty and worth of human nature," Mr. Arnold holds that it "goes beyond religion, as religion is generally conceived among us." For religion, Mr. Arnold thinks, aims at the cultivation of some, and these, no doubt, the highest powers of the soul, at the expense, even at the sacrifice, of other powers, which it regards as lower. So it falls short of that many-sided, even-balanced, all-embracing, totality of development which is the aim of the highest culture.

Mark well this point, for, though I cannot stop to discuss it now, I must return to it after I have set before you Mr. Arnold's view in its further bearings.

After insisting, then, that culture is the study of perfection, harmonious, all-embracing, consisting in becoming something rather than in having something, in an inward condition of soul rather than in any outward circumstances, Mr. Arnold goes on to show how hard a battle culture has to fight in this country, with how many of our strongest tendencies, our most deep-rooted characteristics, it comes into direct, even violent collision. The prominence culture gives to the soul, the inward and spiritual condition, as transcending all outward goods put together, comes into conflict with our worship of a mechanical and material civilization. The social aspirations it calls forth for the general elevation of the human family conflict with our intense individualism, our "every man for himself." The totality of its aim, the harmonious expansion of all human capacities, contradicts our inveterate one-sidedness, our absorption each in his own one pursuit. It conflicts, above all, with the tendency so strong in us to worship the means and to forget the ends of life.

Everywhere, as he looks around him, Mr. Arnold sees this great British people chasing the means of living with unparalleled energy, and forgetting the inward things of our being, which alone give these means their value. We are, in fact, idol-worshippers without knowing it. We worship freedom, the right to do every man as he chooses, careless whether the thing we choose to do be good or not. We worship railroads, steam, coal, as if these made a nation's greatness, forgetting that —

> "by the soul
> Only the nations shall be great and free."

We worship wealth, as men have done in all ages, in spite of the voices of all the wise, only perhaps never before in the world's history with such unanimity, such strength and consistency of devotion, as at this hour, in this land. I must quote the words in which he makes Culture address the mammon-worshippers, those who have either gotten wealth, or, being hot in the pursuit of it, regard wealth and welfare as synonymous : —

"Consider," he makes Culture say, "these people, their way of life, their habits, their manners, the very tones of their voice ; look at them attentively, observe the literature they read (if they read any), the things that give them pleasure, the words which come forth from their mouths, the thoughts which make the furniture of their minds ; would any amount of wealth be worth having with the condition that one was to become like these people by having it? Thus," he says, "culture begets a dissatisfaction which is of the highest possible value in stemming the common tide of men's thoughts in a wealthy and industrious community, and which saves the future, as one may hope, from being wholly materialized and vulgarized, if it cannot save the present." Against all this absorbing faith in machinery, whatever form it takes, whether faith in wealth or in liberty, used or abused, or in coals and railroads, or in bodily health and vigor, or in population, Mr. Arnold lifts up an earnest protest.

It is an old lesson, but one which each age forgets and needs to be taught anew: men forgetting the inward and spiritual goods, and setting their hope on the outward and material ones. Against this all the wise of the earth have, each one in his day, cried aloud, — the philosophers, moralists, and satirists of Greece and Rome, Plato, Epictetus, Seneca, and Juvenal, not less than Hebrew prophets and Christian apostles, up to that Divine voice which said, "What shall it profit a man, if he gain the whole world, and lose his own soul?"

This same old lesson Mr. Arnold repeats,

but in modern language, and turns against the shapes of idol-worship, which he sees everywhere around him.

In contrast, then, to all the grosser interests that absorb us, he pleads for a mental and spiritual perfection, which has two sides, or prominent notes, beauty and intelligence, or, borrowing words which Swift first used, and which, since Mr. Arnold reproduced them, have become proverbial, "Sweetness and Light," — "An inward and spiritual activity having for its characters increased sweetness, increased light, increased life, increased sympathy."

The age of the world in which these two, "sweetness and light," were preëminently combined was, Mr. Arnold thinks, the best age of Athens — that which is represented in the poetry of Sophocles, in whom "the idea of beauty and a full-developed humanity" took to itself a religious and devout energy, in the strength of which it worked. But this was but for a moment of time, when the Athenian mind touched its acme. It was a hint of what might be when the world was ripe for it, rather than a condition which could then continue. In our own countrymen,

Mr. Arnold believes, partly from the toughness and earnestness of the Saxon nature, partly from the predominance in our education of the Hebrew teaching, the moral and religious element has been drawn out too exclusively. There is among us an entire want of the idea of beauty, harmony, and completely rounded human excellence. These ideas are either unknown to us, or entirely misapprehended.

Mr. Arnold then goes on to contrast his idea of a perfectly and harmoniously developed human nature with the idea set up by Puritanism, and prevalent amid our modern multifarious churches. He grants that the church organizations have done much. They have greatly helped to subdue the grosser animalities, — they have made life orderly, moral, serious. But when we go beyond this, and look at the standards of perfection which these religious organizations have held up, he finds them poor and miserable, starving more than a half, and that the finest part of human nature. He turns to modern religious life, as imaged in the *Nonconformist* or some other religious newspaper of the hour, and asks, What do we find there? "A life of jealousy of other churches, disputes, tea meetings, openings of chapels, sermons." And then he exclaims, "Think of this as an ideal of human life, completing itself on all sides, and aspiring with all its organs after sweetness, light, and perfection!" "How," he asks, "is the ideal of a life so unlovely, so unattractive, so narrow, so far removed from a true and satisfying ideal of human perfection, ... to conquer and transform all the vice and hideousness" that we see around us? "Indeed, the strongest plea for the study of perfection as pursued by culture, the clearest proof of the actual inadequacy of the idea of perfection held by the religious organizations, — expressing, as I have said, the most wide-spread effort which the human race has yet made after perfection, — is to be found in the state of our life and society with these in possession of it, and having been in possession of it I know not how many years. We are all of us included in some religious organization or other; we all call ourselves, in the sublime and aspiring language of religion, children of God. Children of God, — it is an immense pretension! — and how are we to justify it? By the works which we do, and the words which we speak. And the work which we collective children of God do, our grand centre of life, our city, is London! London, with its unutterable external hideousness, and with its internal canker, *publicè egestas, privatim opulentia*, unequaled in the world!"

These are severe words, yet they have a side of truth in them. They portray our actual state so truly, that, though they may not be the whole truth, it is well we should remember them, for they cannot be altogether gainsaid.

I have now done with the exposition of Mr. Arnold's theory. Before going on to note what seems to me to be its radical defect, let me first draw attention to two of its most prominent merits.

His pleading for a perfection which consists in a condition of soul, evenly and harmoniously developed, is but a new form of saying, "A man's life consisteth not in the abundance of the things which he possesseth." You will say, perhaps, Is not this a very old truth? Why make such ado about it, as though it were a new discovery? Has it not been expressed far more strongly in the Bible than by Mr. Arnold? True, it is an old truth, and we all know it is in the Bible.

But it is just these old truths which we know so well by the ear, but so little with the heart, that need to be reiterated to each age in the new language which it speaks. The deepest truths are always becoming commonplaces, till they are revivified by thought. And they are true thinkers and benefactors of their kind who, having thought them over once more, and passed them through the alembic of their own hearts, bring them forth fresh-minded, and make them tell anew on their generation. And of all the old proverbs that this age needs applied to it, none is more needed than that which Mr. Arnold has proclaimed so forcibly.

Again, as to the defects which Mr. Arnold charges against our many and divided religious organizations, it cannot be denied that the moral and social results we see around us are far from satisfactory. In this state of things we cannot afford to neglect whatever aid that culture or any other power offers, — to ignore those sides and forces of human nature which, if called into play, might render our ideal at once more complete and more efficient. There is much to excuse the complaints which highly educated men are apt to make, that religious minds have often been satisfied with a very partial and narrow development of humanity, such as does not satisfy, and ought not to satisfy, thoughtful and cultivated men. The wise and truly religious thing to do is not to get angry at such criticisms, and give them bad names, but to be candid, and listen to those who tell us of our shortcomings, — try to see what justice there may be in them, and to turn whatever truth they may contain to good account.

Mr. Arnold sets before us a lofty aim, — he has bid us seek our good in something unseen, in a spiritual energy. In doing this he has done well. But I must hold that he has erred in his estimate of what that spiritual energy is, and he has missed, I think, the true source from which it is to be mainly derived. For in his account of it he has placed that as primary which is secondary and subordinate, and made that secondary which by right ought to be supreme.

You will remember that when describing his idea of the perfection to be aimed at, he makes religion one factor in it, — an important and powerful factor no doubt, still but one element out of several, and that not necessarily the ruling element, but a means towards an end, higher, more supreme, more all-embracing than itself. The end was a many-sided, harmonious development of human nature, and to this end religion was only an important means.

In thus assigning to religion a secondary, however important, place, this theory, as I conceive, if consistently acted on, would annihilate religion. There are things which are either ends in themselves or they are nothing; and such, I conceive, religion is. It either is supreme, a good in itself and for its own sake, or it is not at all. The first and great commandment must either be so set before us as to be obeyed, entered into, in and for itself, without any ulterior view, or it cannot be obeyed at all. It cannot be made subservient to any ulterior purpose. And herein is instanced "a remarkable law of ethics, which is well known to all who have given their minds to the subject." I shall give it in the words of one who has expressed it so well in his own unequaled language that it has been proposed to name it after him, Dr. Newman's law: — "All virtue and goodness tend to make men powerful in this world; but they who aim at the power have not the virtue. Again: Virtue is its own reward, and brings with it the truest and highest pleasures; but they who cultivate it for the pleasure-sake are selfish, not religious, and will never gain the pleasure, because they never can have the virtue."

Apply this to the present subject. They who seek religion for culture-sake are æsthetic, not religious, and will never gain that grace which religion adds to culture, because they never can have the religion. To seek religion for the personal elevation or even for the social improvement it brings, is really to fall from faith which rests in God and the knowledge of Him as the ultimate good, and has no by-ends to serve. And what do we see in actual life? There shall be two men, one of whom has started on the road of self-improvement from a mainly intellectual interest, from the love of art, literature, science, or from the delight these give, but has not been actuated by a sense of responsibility to a Higher than himself. The other has begun with some sense of God, and of his relation to Him, and starting from this centre has gone on to add to it all the moral and mental improvement within his reach, feeling that, beside the pleasure these things give in themselves, he will thus best fulfill the purpose of Him who gave them, thus best promote the good of his fellow-men, and attain the end of his own existence. Which of these two will be the highest man, in which will be gathered up the most excellent graces of character, the truest nobility of soul? You cannot doubt it. The sense that a man is serving a Higher than himself, with a service which will become ever more and more perfect freedom, evokes more profound, more humbling, more exalted emotions than anything else in the world can do. The spirit of man is an instrument which cannot give out its deepest, finest tones, except under the immediate hand of the Divine Harmonist. That is, before it can educe the highest capacities of which human nature is susceptible, culture must cease to be merely culture, and pass over into religion. And here we see another aspect of that great ethical law already noticed as compassing all human action, whereby "the abandoning of some lower object in obedience to a higher aim is made the very condition of securing the said lower object." According to this law it comes that he will approach nearer to perfection, or (since to speak of perfection in such as we are sounds like presumption) rather let us say, he will reach further, will attain to a truer, deeper, more lovely humanity, who makes not culture, but oneness with the will of God, his ultimate aim. The ends of culture, truly conceived, are best attained by forgetting culture, and aiming higher. And what is this but translating into modern and less forcible language the old words, whose meaning is often greatly misunderstood, "Seek ye first the kingdom of God, and all other things will be added unto you?" But by seeking the other things first, as we naturally do, we miss not only the kingdom of God, but those other things also which are only truly attained by aiming beyond them.

Another objection to the theory we have been considering remains to be noted. Its starting-point is the idea of perfecting self; and though, as it gradually evolves, it tries to forget self, and to include quite other elements, yet it never succeeds in getting clear of the taint of self-reference with which it set out. While making this objection, I do not forget that Mr. Arnold, in drawing out his view, proposes as the end of culture to make reason and the kingdom of God prevail; that he sees clearly, and insists strongly, that an isolated self-culture is impossible, that we cannot make progress towards perfection ourselves, unless we strive earnestly to carry our fellow-men along with us. Still may it not with justice be said that these unselfish elements — the desire for others' good, the desire to advance God's kingdom on earth — are in this theory awakened, not simply for their own sakes, not chiefly because they are good in themselves, but because they are clearly discerned to be necessary to our self-perfection, — elements apart from which this cannot exist? And so it comes that culture, though made our end never so earnestly, cannot shelter a man from thoughts about himself, cannot free him from that which all must feel to be fatal to high character, — continual self-consciousness. The only forces strong enough to do this are great truths which carry him out of and beyond himself, the things of the spiritual world sought, not mainly because of their reflex action on us, but for their own sakes, because of their own inherent worthiness. There is perhaps no truer sign that a man is really advancing than that he is learning to forget himself, that he is losing the natural thoughts about self in the thought of One higher than himself, to whose guidance he can commit himself and all men. This is no doubt a lesson not quickly learnt; but there is no help to learning it in theories of self-culture which exalt man's natural self-seeking into a specious and refined philosophy of life.

Again, it would seem that in a world made like ours, Culture, as Mr. Arnold conceives it, instead of becoming an all-embracing bond of brotherhood, is likely to be rather a principle of exclusion and isolation. Culture such as he pictures is at present confessedly the possession of a very small circle. Consider, then, the average powers of men, the circumstances in which the majority must live, the physical wants that must always be uppermost in their thoughts, and say if we can conceive that, even in the most advanced state of education and civilization possible, high culture can become the common portion of the multitude. And with the few on a high level of cultivation, the many, to take the best, on a much lower, what is the natural result? Fastidious exclusiveness on the part of the former, which is hardly human, certainly not Christian. Take any concourse of men, from the House of Commons down to the humblest conventicle, how will the majority of them appear to eyes refined by elaborate culture, but not humanized by any deeper sentiment? To such an onlooker will not the countenances of most seem unlovely, their manners repulsive, their modes of thought commonplace, — it may be, sordid? By any such concourse the man of mere culture will, I think, feel himself repelled, not attracted. So it must be, because Culture, being mainly a literary and æsthetic product, finds little in the unlettered multitude that is akin to itself. It is, after all, a dainty and divisive quality, and cannot reach to the depths of humanity. To do this takes some deeper, broader, more brotherly impulse, one which shall touch the universal ground on which men are one, not that in which they differ, — their common nature, common destiny, the needs that poor and rich alike share. For this we must look elsewhere than to Culture, however enlarged.

The view I have been enforcing will appear more evident if from abstract arguments we turn to the actual lives of men. Take any of the highest examples of our race, those who have made all future generations their debtors. Can we imagine any of these being content to set before themselves, merely as the end of their endeavors, such an aim as the harmonious development of human nature? A Goethe perhaps might, and if we take him as the highest, we will take his theory likewise. Hardly, I think, Shakespeare, if we can conceive of him as ever having set before himself consciously any formal aim. But could we imagine St. Paul doing so, or Augustine, or Luther, or such men as Pascal or Archbishop Leighton? Would such a theory truly represent the ends they lived for, the powers that actuated them, the ideal whence they drew their strength? These men changed the moral orbit of the world, but by what lever did they change it? Not by seeking their own perfection, nor even by making the progress of the race their only aim. They found a higher, more permanent world on which to plant the lever that was to move this one. They sought first the advancement of the kingdom of God and truth for its own sake, and they knew that this embraced the true good of man and every other good thing.

Indeed, of Culture put in the supreme place, it has been well said that it holds forth a hope for humanity by enlightening self, and not a hope for humanity by dying to self. This last is the hope which Christianity sets before us. It teaches, what indeed human experience in the long-run teaches too, that man's chief good lies in ceasing from the Individual Self, that he may live in a higher Personality, in whose purpose all the ends of our true Personality are secure. The sayings in the Gospels to this effect will readily occur to every one. Some glimpse of the same truth had visited the mind of the speculative Greek poet four hundred years before the Christian era, when he said: —

> Τίς οἶδεν εἰ τὸ ζῆν μέν ἐστι κατθανεῖν,
> Τὸ κατθανεῖν δὲ ζῆν;
>
> "Who knoweth whether life may not be death,
> And death itself be life?"

There is but one other thought I would submit to you. Those who build their chief hope for humanity on Culture rather than on Religion would raise men by bringing them into contact and sympathy with whatever of best and greatest the past has produced. But is not a large portion of what is best in the literature and the lives of past generations based on faith in God, and on the reality of communion with Him as the first and chief good? Would this best any longer live and grow in men if you cut them off from direct access to its fountain-head, and confined them to the results which it has produced in past ages, — if, in fact, you made the object of the soul's contemplation not God, but past humanity? Are we of these latter days to be content with the results of the communion of others, and not have direct access to it ourselves, — to read and admire the high thoughts of à Kempis, Pascal, Leighton, and such men, and not to go on and drink for ourselves from the same living well-heads from which they drank? Not now, any more than in past ages, can the most be made of human character, even in this life, till we ascend above humanity, —

"Unless above himself he can
Erect himself, how mean a thing is man!"

I cannot close without expressing a feeling which I dare say has been present to the minds of many here, as throughout this lecture they listened to the oft-repeated word *perfection*. Perfection! the very word seems like mockery when applied to such as we. For how poor a thing must any perfection be that is reached this side the grave! Far truer is that word of St. Augustine, — "That is the true perfection of a man, to find out his own imperfection." Yes, the highest perfection any one will attain in this life is to be ever increasingly sensible how imperfect he is. As perfection is put forward in the theory I have been examining, one cannot but feel that there is a very inadequate notion of the evil in the human heart that is to be cured, and of the nature of the powers that are needed to cope with it. And in this respect we cannot but be struck with how greatly Christianity differs from Culture, and differs only to surpass it: its estimate of the disease is so much deeper, and the remedy to which it turns so far transcends all human nostrums. Christianity, too, holds out perfection as the goal. But in doing so its view is not confined to time, but contemplates an endless progression in far-on ages. The perfection the Culturists speak of, if it does not wholly exclude the other life, seems to fix the eye mainly on what can be done here, and not to take much account of what is beyond. That was a higher and truer idea of perfection which Leighton had: "It is an union with a Higher Good by love, that alone is endless perfection. The only sufficient object for man must be something that adds to and perfects his nature, to which he must be united in love; somewhat higher than himself, yea, the highest of all, the Father of spirits. That alone completes a spirit and blesses it, — to love Him, the spring of spirits."

To sum up all that has been said, the defect in Mr. Arnold's theory is this: It places in the second and subordinate place that which should be supreme, and elevates to the position of command a power which, rightly understood, should be subordinate and ministrant to a higher than itself. The relation to God is first, this relation is last, and Culture should fill up the interspace, — Culture, that is, the endeavor to know and use aright the nature which He has given us, and the world in which He has placed us. Used in such a way, Culture is transmuted into something far higher, more beneficent, than it ever could become if it set up for itself and claimed the chief place.

I might now conclude, but there is a poem of Archbishop Trench's, one of his earliest, and most interesting, which so well embodies much that I have said, that I hope you will bear with me while I read a somewhat lengthy passage from it. The lines are simple, not greatly elaborated, but they are true, and they may perhaps fix the attention of some who by this time have grown weary of abstract and prosaic argument, — according to that saying, —

"A verse may find him who a sermon flies."

A youth, a favored child of Culture, when he has long sought and not found what he expected to find in Culture, wanders forth desolate and desponding into the eastern desert. *The irrevocable past lies heavy* on him, — his baffled purpose, his wasted years, his utter misery. So heart-forlorn is he that he is on the verge of self-destruction. At length, as he sits inconsolable beside a ruined temple in the desert, an old man stands by his side, and asks, "What is your sorrow ?" The youth, lured by some strange sympathy in the old man's mien and voice, unburdens to him his grief, tells how he has tried to make and keep himself wise and pure and elevated above the common crowd, that in his soul's mirror he might find

"A reflex of the eternal mind,
A glass to give him back the truth,"

how he has followed after ideal beauty, to live in its light, dwell beneath its shadow, but at length has found that this too is vanity and emptiness.

"Till now, my youth yet scarcely done,
The heart which I had thought to steep
In hues of beauty, and to keep
Its consecrated home and fane,
That heart is soiled with many a stain,
Which from without or from within
Has gathered there till all is sin,
Till now I only draw my breath,
I live but in the hope of death."

After an interval the old man replies,

"Ah me, my son,
A weary course your life has run;
And yet it need not be in vain
That you have suffered all this pain; . .
Nay, deem not of us as at strife,
Because you set before your life
A purpose, and a loftier aim
Than the blind lives of men may claim
For the most part; or that you sought,
By fixed resolve and solemn thought,
To lift your being's calm estate
Out of the range of time and fate.
Glad am I that a thing unseen,
A spiritual Presence, this has been
Your worship, this your young heart stirred.
But yet herein you proudly erred,
Here may the source of woe be found,
You thought to fling yourself around
The atmosphere of light and love
In which it was your joy to move;
You thought by efforts of your own
To take at last each jarring tone
Out of your life, till all should meet
In one majestic music sweet;
And deemed that in your own heart's ground
The root of good was to be found,
And that by careful watering
And earnest tendance we might bring

The bud, the blossom, and the fruit,
To grow and flourish from that root.
You deemed you needed nothing more
Than skill and courage to explore
Deep down enough in your own heart,
To where the well-head lay apart,
Which must the springs of being feed,
And that these fountains did but need
The soil that choked them moved away,
To bubble in the open day.
But thanks to Heaven it is not so:
That root a richer soil doth know
Than our poor hearts could e'er supply; —
That stream is from a source more high;
From God it came, to God returns,
Not nourished from our scanty urns,
But fed from His unfailing river,
Which runs and will run on forever."

LECTURE IV.

HINDRANCES TO SPIRITUAL GROWTH.

It has often happened that when the sons of a family, after having been for some ses sions at College, have returned to their own homes, bursars, or scholars, or M. A.'s with honors, the family have felt that somehow they were changed, had lost their old simple natures, and for this loss college learning and distinctions seemed but a poor substitute. This, however, may be only a temporary result of severe mental tension and seclusion. When the bow has been for a time unstrung, the unnaturalness passes, and the native, simple self reappears.

But I have known other stories than these. I have heard of devout and self-denying parents, working late and early, and stinting themselves to send their sons to College, and in sending them their fond hope was that these young men would return stored with knowledge and wisdom, and be able to help their parents in those religious subjects on which their hearts were most set. Such hopes, we may trust, have many times been realized. But one has heard of cases which had another issue. A young man has come home, after a college course, acute, logical, speculative, full of the newest views, prating of high matters, scientific and philosophical, a very *prodigy of enlightenment.* But that on which early piety had fed was forsaken, the old reverence was gone, and the parents saw, with helpless sorrow, that their son had chosen for himself a far other road than that on which they were travelling, and in which they had hoped he would travel with them.

It is a common tale, one which has often been repeated, but none the less pathetic for that. It brings before us the collision that often occurs when newly awakened intellect first meets with early faith. No one who has observed men ever so little but must know something, either through his own experience or from watching others, of these travail-pangs that often accompany the birth of thought.

The special trial of each spirit lies in that very field in which his strength and activity are put forth. The temptation of the busy trader does not consist in mental questionings, but in the tendency to inordinate love of gain. The æsthetic spirit finds its trial, not in coarse pleasures, but in the temptation to follow beauty exclusively, and to turn effeminately from duty and self-denial. And in like manner the student or man of letters will most likely find his trial in dealing rightly with the intellectual side of things, giving to it its due place, and not more. What are some of the difficulties and temptations which the student is apt to meet with, and which may be the best way to deal with them, — this is the subject which will engage us to-day. Before entering on it, however, let me say distinctly that I do not believe that painful questionings and violent mental convulsions are an ordeal which all thoughtful persons must needs pass through. So far from this, some of the finest spirits, those whose vision is most intuitive and penetrating, are the most exempt from such anxious soul-travail. Indeed, I believe that there is no such safeguard against the worst consequences of such perplexities as a heart that is pure, humble, and "at leisure from itself." In the words of a modern divine, one well known at the present time, both as an upholder of freedom of inquiry, and also as a religious and devoted man, —

"There are some who are never troubled with doubts at all. They live so heavenly a life that doubts and perplexities fall off their minds without fastening. They find enough in their faith to feed their spiritual life. They do not need to inquire into the foundations of their belief, they are inspired by a power within their hearts. The heavenly side of all truths is so clear to them that any doubts about the human form of it are either unintelligible or else at once rejected. They grow in knowledge by quiet, steady increase of light, without any intervals of darkness and difficulty. This is the most blessed state, — that of those who can believe without the evidence either of sense or of labored argument. There are such minds. There are those to whom the inward proof is everything. They believe not on the evidence of their senses, or of their mere reason, but on that of their consciences and hearts. Their spirits within them are so attuned to the truth that the moment it is presented to them they accept it at once. And this is certainly the higher state, the more blessed, the more heavenly."

These are they who have always rejoiced in a serene, unclouded vision till they are taken home. And we have known such.

Let none, therefore, pique themselves on having doubts and questionings on religious subjects, as if it were a fine thing to have them, proving them to be intellectual athletes, and entitling them to look down on those who are free from them as inferior persons, less mentally gifted. For there is a higher state than their own — there is a purer atmosphere, which has been breathed by persons of as strong intellect as themselves, but of a finer spirit. But such is not the state of all thoughtful men. There are many who when they reach the reasoning age find themselves in the midst of many difficulties, hedged in with "perplexities which they cannot explain to themselves, much less to others, and no one to help them." They are afraid to tell their sad heart-secrets to others, and especially to their elders, lest they find no sympathy. And so they are tempted to shut them up within their own breasts, and brood over them till they get morbid and magnify their difficulties out of all proportion to their reality. In the case of such persons it becomes a serious question how they should be advised to treat the difficulties that occur to them. On the one hand, while they are not to make little questions of great consequence, neither must they make grave questions and perplexities of little consequence. They are to be told that while all doubts are painful, all are not necessarily wrong. For some are natural, born of honesty, and, when rightly dealt with, have often ere now become the birth-pangs of larger knowledge, — the straits through which men passed to clearer light. There are, on the other hand, doubts which are sinful, born of levity, irreverence, and self-conceit, or of a hard and perverted conscience. To determine to which class any particular mental perplexities belong is not easy for a man even in his own case; much more is it difficult, nay impossible, for us to read the mental state of another, and pronounce judgment on it. The fact that some doubts are not sinless, that they may arise out of the state of a man's spirit, suggests to every one cautiousness and self-scrutiny. This is a work which no man can do for his brother. Each man must take his own difficulties into the light of conscience and of God, and there deal with them honestly yet humbly, seeking to be guided aright.

For the spirit of a man is a very delicate instrument, which, if it be distorted out of its natural course, this way or that, by prejudice or interest or double-dealing on the one hand, or fool-hardiness and self-confidence on the other, may never perhaps in this life recover its equilibrium.

I should be loath to seem to trespass either on the speculative field of the theological professor, or on the practical one of the Christian minister. But, without doing either, there is room enough for offering such suggestions as have been gathered from a number of years not unobservant of what has been going on in that border land where faith and knowledge meet. To young and ardent spirits the wrestling with hard questions on the very verge of human knowledge has a wonderful fascination. They throw themselves fearlessly into the abyss, and think that they shall be able to dive down to depths hitherto unsounded. Problems that have baffled the world's best thinkers will, they fancy, yield up to them their secret. Yet these things "do take a sober coloring" from eyes which have seen too many young men, some of them the finest spirits of our time, setting forth in over-confidence in their own powers, imagining that they were sufficient to meet all difficulties, and coming before long to mournful shipwreck. When experience has impressed us with the full importance of the mental tendencies for good and for evil which often begin at College, who would not be earnestly disposed to turn his experience, if he might, to the help of those younger than himself, at that interesting time of life when they most need help, and often least find it? But then there comes upon the mind the conviction that this is an issue wherein, in the last resort, no one can bear his brother's burden. All that we can do is to suggest certain dangers to which the student is from the nature of his occupations peculiarly exposed, and to leave it to each for himself to apply what is said conscientiously, according as he feels that it bears on his need.

I. The first hindrance I will notice is one which arises out of the very nature of mental cultivation. If there is one thing which more than another distinguishes a well-trained mind, it is the power of thinking clearly, of dividing with a sharp line between its knowledge and its ignorance. One of the best results of a logical and also of a scientific discipline is that it leads us to form definite, clearly cut conceptions of things. Indeed, this power of limiting, defining, making a ὅρος or bound round each object you think of, and thus making them thinkable, is of the very essence of thought. For what is all thought but a rescuing, a cutting off by the mind's inherent power of bounding, objects from out the vague and undefined? But this quality of all thought, which in trained thought is raised to a higher power, while it constitutes mental strength, contains also its own weakness, or rather limitation. Clearly defined knowledge is mainly of things we see. All find it much easier to form definite conceptions of objects of the outer sense than of objects of the inner sense, — to conceive clearly things we see, hear, and touch, than those thoughts which have not any outward object corresponding to them. If thoughts are difficult adequately to grasp, much more are emotions, —with their infinite complexity, their evanescent shades. But each man gains a power of realizing and firmly conceiving those things he habitually deals with, and not other things. The man whose training has lain exclusively in physics, accurately conceives physical forces, however subtle, and can lay down their relations to each other; but then he will probably be comparatively weak in apprehending subtleties of thought and mental relations. Again, the mere logician, while strong to grasp logical distinctions, will generally be found comparatively at sea when he has to catch the imaginative aspects of things, and fix evanescent hues of feeling. This takes something of the poetic faculty. Each man is strong in that he is trained in, weak in other regions, — so much so that often the objects there seem to him non-existent.

Now the scientific mind and the logical mind, when turned towards the supersensible world, are apt to find the same difficulty, only in a much greater degree, as they find in dealing with objects of imagination, or with pure emotions. Whoever has tried to think steadily at all on religious subjects must be aware of this difficulty. When we look upward, and try to think of God and of the soul's relation to Him, we are apt to feel as if we had stepped out into a world in which the understanding finds little or no firm footing. We cannot present to ourselves these truths adequately, and as they really are.

Therefore we are under the necessity of "substituting anthropomorphic conceptions, determined by accidents of place and time, — to speak of God as dwelling above, to attribute a before and an after to the Divine thought." With these feeble adumbrations, which are the nearest approaches to the reality we can make, the devout mind is content, feeling them to be full of meaning. But the scientific and the logical mind often feels great difficulty in being content with these. It craves more exactness of outline, and is tempted to reject as non-existent things which it cannot subject to the laws of thought to which it is accustomed, — in fact, to limit the orb of belief to the orb of exact knowledge. Mere adumbrations of spiritual realities are an offense to the mind that will accept only scientific exactness. The falsity of this way of reasoning has been well exposed by Coleridge, where he protests against "the application of deductive and conclusive logic to subjects concerning which the premises are expressed in not merely inadequate but accommodated terms. But to conclude terms proper and adequate from quasific and mendicant premises is illogical logic with a vengeance. Water cannot rise higher than its source, neither can human reasoning."

The fact is, those root-truths, on which the foundations of our being rest, are apprehended not logically at all, but mystically. This faculty of spiritual apprehension, which is a very different one from those which are trained in schools and colleges, must be educated and fed, not less but more carefully than our lower faculties, else it will be starved and die, however learned or able in other respects we may become. And the means which train it are reverent thought, meditation, prayer, and all those other means by which the divine life is fed.

But because the primary truths of religion refuse to be caught in the grip of the logical vice, — because they are, as I said, transcendent, and only mystically apprehended, — are thinking men therefore either to give up these objects as impossible to think about, or to content themselves with a vague religiosity, an unreal sentimentalism? Not so. There are certain veritable facts of consciousness to which religion makes its appeal. These the thinking man must endeavor to apprehend with as much definiteness as their nature admits of, — must verify them by his own inward experience, and by the recorded experience of the most religious men. And there are other facts outside of our consciousness and above it, which are revealed that they may fit into and be taken up by those needs of which we are conscious. Rightly to apprehend them, so that we shall make them our own inwardly, so that they shall supplement, deepen, and expand our moral perceptions, not contradict and traverse them, this is no easy work. It is the work of the reflective side of the religious life. But when all is done, it will still remain, that in the whole process intellect or the mere understanding is but a subordinate agent, and must be kept so. The primary agent, on our side, is that power of spiritual apprehension which we know under many names, none perhaps better than those old ones, "the hearing ear, the understanding heart." The main condition is that the spiritual ear should be open to overhear and patiently take in, and the will ready to obey, that testimony which, I believe, God bears in every human heart, however dull, to those great truths which the Bible reveals. This, and not logic, is the way to grow in religious knowledge, to know that the truths of religion are not shadows, but deep realities.

II. Akin to the desire for exact conceptions is the desire for system. The longing to systematize, to form a completely rounded theory of the universe, which shall embrace all known facts, and assign to each its proper place, this craving lies deep in the intellectual man. It is at the root of science and of philosophy in its widest sense: out of it has arisen the whole fabric of exact and scientific knowledge. But this, like other good tendencies, may be overdone, and become rash and one-sided. From this impulse, too hastily carried out, arise such theories of life as that of Professor Huxley, which was discussed in a former lecture. It is this that gives to Positivism the charm it has for many energetic minds. It seems such gain to reach a comprehensive, all-embracing point of view, from which all knowledge shall be seen mapped out, every object and science falling into its proper place, and all uncertainty, all cloudy horizons, rigorously shut out. To many minds, nothing seems too great a price to pay for this. And to secure it, they have to pay a great price. They have to cut off unspairingly all the ragged rims of knowledge, to exclude from view the whole border land between the definitely conceived and the dimly apprehended, — the very region in which the main difficulties of thought peculiarly lie. They have to shut their eyes to all those phenomena, often the most interesting, which they cannot locate. But though such systematizers exclude them from their system, they cannot exclude them from reality. There they remain rooted all the same, whether we recognize them or not. Shut them out as you may, they will, in spite of all theories, reappear, cropping out in human history and in human consciousness. Now it so happens that of these facts which refuse to be systematized, a large part, but by no means all, arise out of man's religious nature. The existence of evil, manifesting itself in man's consciousness as the sense of sin, or estrangement from God, recovery from this, not by any power evolved from man's own resources, but by a power which descended from above, when "heaven opened itself anew to man's long-alienated race," — these, and all the facts they imply, are, and always have been, a stumbling-block to those who are bent on a rounded system. Hence every age, and this age preeminently, has seen attempts to resolve Christianity into a natural product. Because it enters into all things human, and moulds them to itself, the attempt is made to account for it by the joint action of those spiritual elements which preëxisted in human nature. Such attempts Christianity has for eighteen centuries withstood, and will withstand till the end. The idea of a power coming down from a higher sphere to work in and renew the natural forces of humanity, must always be repugnant to any mode of thought which makes a complete system the first necessity. No doubt the craving for a system is a deep instinct of the purely intellectual man, but it is a very different thing from the craving for rightness with God, which is the prime instinct of the spiritual man. When once awakened, the spiritual faculty far outgoes all systems, scientific, philosophic, or theological, and apprehends and lives by truths which these cannot reduce to system.

III. Again, there is another way in which thought seems often to get caught in its own meshes, and so fall short of the highest truth. There is a tendency, not peculiar to the present day, though very prevalent now, to rest in Law, whether in the natural or moral world, and to shrink from going beyond it up to God. There are those who think that when science has ascended to the most general uniformities of sequence and coexistence, then knowledge has reached its limit, and all beyond is mere conjecture. To this I will not reply, in the old phrase, about a law and a law-giver, for this to some seems a play on words. But one thing, often said before, must be repeated. This supposed necessity to rest in the perception of ordered phenomena, is no necessity at all, but an artificial and arbitrarily imposed limitation, against which thought left to its natural action rebels. It is impossible for any reflective mind, not dominated by a system, to regard the ordered array of physical forces, and to rest satisfied with this order, without going on to ask whence it came, what placed it there. Thought cannot be kept back, when it sees arrangement, from asking what is the arranging power; when it sees existence, from inquiry how it came to exist. And the question is a natural and legitimate one, in spite of all that phenomenalism may say against it, and it will not cease to be asked while there are reasoning men to ask it.

The same habit of mind is fain, in moral subjects, to rest in moral law. But, if we look closely at reality, what are moral law, moral order, but abstractions generalized from facts felt and observed by all men? They are not self-subsisting entities, such as our own personality is. And a living will would be justified in refusing allegiance to a mere abstraction, however high or seemingly imperative, if there was nothing behind it. It is because moral law is but a condensed expression for the energy of, shall I say, a Higher Personality, or something greater, more living, more all-encompassing, than personality, that it comes home to us with the power it does.

These are but a few of the more obvious ways in which our intellectual habits may, and often do, become a hindrance instead of a help towards spiritual progress. There are many other ways, more subtle and hard to deal with, some of which I had intended to notice. But for to-day you have probably had enough of abstractions. And what remains of our time must be given to more practical considerations.

Religious men are always trying to set forth in defense of their faith demonstrations which shall be irrefragable. This is natural, nor do I say that it is altogether unwise.

For as facts and doctrines form the intellectual outworks of faith, historical criticism must make good the one, sound philosophy must so far warrant the other. But when all that argument can do has been done, it still remains true that the best and most convincing grounds of faith will still remain behind unshaped into argument. There is a great reserve fund of conviction arising from the increased experience which Christian men have of the truth of what they believe. And this cannot be beat out into syllogisms. It is something too inward, too personal, too mystical, to be set forth so.[1] It is not on that account the less real and powerful. Indeed, it may be said that once felt it is the most self-evidencing of all proofs. This is what Coleridge said, "If you wish to be assured of the truth of Christianity, try it." "Believe, and if thy belief be right, that insight which gradually transmutes faith into knowledge will be the reward of thy belief." To be vitally convinced of the truth of "the process of renewal described by Scripture, a man must put himself within that process." His own experience of its truth, and the confident assurances of others, whom, if candid,

[1] Note VI.

he will feel to be better than himself, will be the most sufficing evidence. But this is an evidence which, while it satisfies a man's self, cannot be brought to bear on those who stand without the pale, and deny those things of which they have not themselves experience.

Many are apt to imagine that a hard head and a blameless deportment make a man free of the inner shrine of Christian truth. When a scholar goes forth from college well equipped with the newest methods, he sometimes fancies that he holds the key to which all the secrets of faith must open. And if they do not at once yield to his mental efforts, he is tempted to regard them as untrue. But clear and trained intellect is one thing, spiritual discernment quite another. The former does not exclude, but neither does it necessarily include the latter. They are energies of two different sides of our being. Unless the spiritual nature in a man is alive and active, it is in vain that he works at religious truth merely from the intellectual side. If he is not awake in a deeper region than his intellectual, though he may be an able critic or dialectician, a vital theologian or a religious man he cannot be. Not long ago I read this remark of the German theologian Rothe, — "It is only the pious subject that can speculate theologically. And why? Because it is he alone who has the original datum, in virtue of communion with God on which the dialectic lays hold. So soon as the original datum is there, everything else becomes simply a matter of logic." Or as a thoughtful English scholar and divine lately expressed it: — "Of all qualities which a theologian must possess, a devotional spirit is the chief. For the soul is larger than the mind, and the religious emotions lay hold on the truths to which they are related on many sides at once. A powerful understanding, on the other hand, seizes on single points, and however enlarged in its own sphere, is of itself never safe from narrowness of view. For its very office is to analyze, which implies that thought is fixed down to particular relations of the subject. No mental conception, still more no expression in words, can give the full significance of any fact, least of all of a divine fact. Hence it is that mere reasoning is found such an ineffectual measure against simple piety, and devotion is such a safeguard against intellectual errors." Yes, "the original datum," that is the main thing.

And what is this but that which our old Puritan forefathers meant when they spoke of a man "having the root of the matter in him?" The devout spirit is not fed by purely intellectual processes, — sometimes it is even frustrated by them. The hard brain-work and the seclusion of the student tend, if uncounteracted, to dry up the springs alike of the human sympathies and of the heavenward emotions. It was a saying of Dr. Arnold, certainly no disparager of intellect, that no student could continue long in a healthy religious state unless his heart was kept tender by mingling with children, or by frequent intercourse with the poor and the suffering.

And this suggests a subject which might occupy a whole lecture or course of lectures, to which, however, now only a few words can be given. It is one main object of all our education here to train the critical faculty. This faculty, educated by scholarship, has an important function to fill in matters bearing on religion. With regard to these it has a work to do which ought not to be disregarded, and that work it is at present doing actively enough. To weigh evidence, and form a sound judgment whether alleged facts are really true, whether documents really belong to the age and the authors they profess to be of,— by trained historical imagination to enter into the whole circumstances and meaning of any past age, — to examine the meaning of the Sacred Scriptures, and see "how far its modes and figures of representation are merely vehicles of inner truth, or are of the essence of the truth itself, — to understand the human conditions of the writers, and appreciate how far these may have influenced their statements, — to give to past theological language its proper weight, and not more than its proper weight, — to trace the history of its terms so as not to confound human thought with divine faith," — all these processes are essential to the theologian, — some measure of them is required in every educated man who will think rightly on such subjects. I would not underrate the value of this kind of work. It is necessary in the educated, if well-grounded religion is to live among the people, and faith is not to be wholly dissevered from intellectual truth. At the same time it is carried on in the outworks rather than in the citadel, it deals with the shells rather than with the kernel of divine things. This vocation of the critic, however useful for others, has dangers for himself. There is a risk that criticism shall absorb his whole being. This is no imaginary danger. We are not called on to believe this or that doctrine which may be proposed to us till we can do so from honest conviction. But we are called on to trust, — to trust ourselves to God, being sure that He will lead us right, — to keep close to Him, — and to trust the promises which He whispers through our conscience; this we can do, and we ought to do. Every scholar who is also a religious man must have felt it, — must be aware how apt he is to approach the simplest spiritual truths as a critic, not as a simple learner. And yet he feels that when all is said and done, it is trust, not criticism, that the soul lives by. If he is ever to get beyond the mere outer precinct and pass within the holy place, he must put off his critical apparatus, and enter as a simple contrite-hearted man. Not as men of science, not as critics, not as philosophers, but as little children, shall we enter into the kingdom of heaven. "Therefore," says Leighton, speaking of filial prayer, "many a poor unlettered Christian far outstrips your school rabbis in this attainment, because it is not effectually taught in these lower academies."

These are reflections needed perhaps at all times by those immersed in thought and study, — never more needed than now. Numberless voices, through newspaper, pamphlet, periodical, from platform and pulpit, are telling us that we are in the midst of a transition age, so loudly that the dullest cannot choose but hear. It is a busy, restless time, eager to cast off the old and reach forward to the new. It needs no diviner to tell us that this century will not pass without a great breaking up of the dogmatic structures that have held ever since the Reformation or the succeeding age. From many sides at once a simplifying of the code, a revision of the standards, is being demanded. I will not ask whether this is good or bad, desirable or not. It is enough that it is inevitable. From such a removal of old landmarks two opposite results may arise. Either it may make faith easier by taking cumbrous forms out of the way, — it may make the direct approach to Christ and God simple and more natural, — may, in fact, bring God nearer to the souls of men, — or it may remove Him to a greater distance, and make life more completely secular. Which shall the result be? This depends for each of us on the way we use the new state of things, on the preparedness or non-preparedness of heart with which we meet it. Often it is seen that great changes, which in the long-run turn to the good of the community, bring suffering and grievous loss on their way to many an individual. And a time of transition, when the old bonds are being broken up, is a time of trial to the spirits of men. At such a time, in anxiety but not in despair, we ask, how is the old piety to live on through all changes into the new world that is to be? If the outward framework that helped to strengthen our fathers is being removed, the more the need that we should cleave to the inward, the vital, the spiritual communion with Him on whom the soul lives. Secular and worldly common sense will discuss in newspapers, literary criticism in magazines, these momentous changes; but such talk touches only the outside aspect of them, and cannot discern what is essential or what is not. Even refined intellectuality cannot much help us here. That which passes safely through all changes is the tender conscience, the trusting heart, the devout mind. Let us seek these, and the disciplines which strengthen them. College learning is good, but not all the learning of all the Universities of Europe can compensate for the loss of that which the youth reared in a religious home has learned in childhood at his mother's knee.

In all the best men you meet, perhaps the thing that is most peculiar about them is the child's heart they bear within the man's. However they have differed in other respects, in their tempers, gifts, attainments, in this they agreed. With those things they were, so to speak, clothed upon, — this was their very core, their essential self. And this child's heart it is that is the organ of faith, trust, heavenly communion. It is a very simple thing, so simple that worldly men are apt either not to perceive or to despise it. And young persons when they first grow up, and enter the world, are tempted to make little of it. They think that now they are men they must put away childish things, must learn the world, and conform to its ways and estimates of things.

But the τὰ τοῦ νηπίου, the childish things, which St. Paul put away, belong to a quite different side of child-nature from the παιδίον, the little child which our Lord recommended for our example.

We should try, as we grow up into manhood, and get to know the world, to have this simplicity of childhood kept fresh within us, still at the centre. If we allow the world to rob us of it, as so many do, in boyhood, even before manhood begins, we may be sure that the world has nothing equal to it to give us instead. And they who may have for a time lost it, or had it obscured or put into abeyance by contact with men, cannot too soon seek to have it restored within them. And the only way to preserve this good thing, or have it, if lost, renewed, is to open the heart to simple, truthful communion with God and Christ, and try to bring the heart ever closer and closer to Him.

That this is intended to be our very inmost nature, the way in which we are reared by Providence seems to show. For all the first years of our life He surrounds us with the warm charities of home, — by these He calls out all our earliest, deepest, most permanent feelings. School, college, the world follow, but their influences, great as they are, never penetrate down, at least in natural characters, so deep as those first affections. And then in mature life, the home of childhood is generally, if possible, reproduced in a home of our own, in which all the early affections are once more renewed, enhanced by the thoughtfulness that life has brought.

Let me close with reading what Pascal has left as his Profession of Faith: —

"I love poverty, because Jesus Christ loved it. I love wealth, because it gives me the means of assisting the wretched. I keep faith with all men. I do not render evil to those who do it to me; but I desire a state for them like to my own, in which I receive neither evil nor good from the hand of man. I endeavor to be just, truthful, sincere, and faithful to all men; and I have a tenderness of heart for those to whom God has united me more closely; and whether I am alone, or in the sight of men, in all my actions I have in sight God, who must judge them, and to whom I have consecrated them all.

"These are my sentiments, and I bless all the days of my life my Redeemer, who has put them into me, and who, from a man full of weakness, misery, concupiscence, pride, and ambition, has made a man exempt from all these evils by the strength of His grace, to which all the glory of it is due, since I have in myself nothing but misery and error."

LECTURE V.

RELIGION COMBINING CULTURE WITH ITSELF.

THE truth which I tried to bring before you in my last lecture, though a very obvious one, is yet sometimes forgotten. It was this: To discern and judge rightly of spiritual truth is not mainly the work of the logical understanding, nor of rough and round common sense. To do this requires that another capacity be awake in a man, — a spiritual apprehension, or, call it by what name you may, a deeper, more internal light, which shall be behind the understanding, as it were, informing and illuminating it. For otherwise the understanding, however powerful or acute, attains not to spiritual truth. This power of spiritual apprehension we saw is, though not identical with the moral nature, more akin to it, — belongs more to this side of our being than to the intellectual. It contains the moral nature, and something more than what ordinarily comes under that name. Like every other power in man, it is capable of growth and cultivation. We can, if we choose, starve and kill it, or we can, by submitting it to its proper discipline and bringing it into contact with its proper objects, deepen and expand it. Care, watchfulness, earnest cultivation it requires; but that cultivation is of a different kind, as its objects are different, from that which trains the intellect and the imagination, and it cannot be directly taught in colleges and schools.

The belief that the spiritual faculty is different from the logical and scientific faculty, led me to notice some of the hindrances which our habits as students often put in the way of spiritual vision and religious growth. The mental tendencies which I noted were among the most obvious, those that meet us at the very threshold. There are several others more recondite, which I should have liked to notice; but to this branch of the subject enough of time has been given. The more welcome task awaits me to-day of speaking for a little, not of the hindrances, but of the helps towards spiritual knowledge.

The capacity of spiritual apprehension — that is, the power to apprehend spiritual truths — is, I believe, latent in all men.

Persons differ in the amount of their capacity, or rather in their readiness to receive or to reject these things; but that the capacity is in all men, dim, almost dormant it may be, yet really there incipiently, one cannot doubt. Whether these latent elements shall grow and live and become powerful within us, or be stifled, crushed, extinguished, depends in some measure on circumstances which we cannot control, — such as our home training, our companions, our education, our temptations; but in some large measure also it depends on our own choice.

Since this is so, since so much lies in our power as to what we shall actually become in this the deepest part of our being, it becomes an important inquiry how we ought to deal each with ourselves, and how we can best help others in this respect.

First, then, it is quite certain that if from childhood men were to begin to follow the first intimations of conscience, honestly to obey them and carry them out into act, the power of conscience would be so strengthened and improved within them, that it would soon become, what it evidently is intended to be, "a connecting principle between the creature and the Creator." This light that lighteth every man, if any were to follow it consistently, would soon lead a man up and on to a clear and full knowledge of God, and to the formation of the Divine image within himself. But none do so follow these heavenward promptings, all more or less disobey them, thwart them, and so dim and distort their spiritual light. A few there are, however, who, though not free from the inborn obliquity, do begin, earlier than most men, to cherish conscience, and, with whatever declensions, do on the whole make it their main endeavor to obey it. And these are led on quickly and early to the serener heights whence they see spiritual truths more clearly, vividly, and abidingly than ordinary men. But this is not the case with the most. Even those who may never have fallen into open and flagrant sin, have yet made not duty but inclination their first guide, have tried to strike innumerable compromises between self-pleasing and duty, in which self has had much the best of the bargain, — have at best tried "to please themselves without displeasing God." And so by going on in this self-deceiving, double-minded way, they have weakened not strengthened, dimmed not brightened, the original light that was within them. So conscience has not to them been an open avenue of communication upward, a direct access to God.

Without, however, dwelling on the innumerable shades and ways of declension, one thing remains true for all. Whatever our past life may have been, at whatever point of life and progress we may be standing, if we would not destroy what we have still left of spiritual apprehension, if we have any desire to grow in spiritual growth, the first thing to be done is to face conscience, — to be entirely honest with ourselves, to cease from excusing ourselves to ourselves, cease from subterfuges and self-deceptions, and bring ourselves, our desires, our past lives, our aims, our characters into the light of conscience and of God, and there desire to have them searched, sifted, cleansed.

To be thus perfectly single-hearted and candid is, I know, a most difficult attainment. Entire candor and honesty regarding ourselves, instead of being the first, is one of the last and highest attainments of a perfectly fashioned character. But though this is true, it is also the beginning of all well-doing; without some measure of it, even though weak and unsteady, no good thing can begin.

We must be honest with ourselves, desire to know the truth about ourselves, desire, however faintly, to be better than we are, or there is no bettering possible for us. But if this desire is in us, it is the germ out of which all good may come. The first honest acting out of this desire will be to face conscience, as I said, to walk according to the light we have, to do the immediate thing we know to be right, and then more light will follow. We shall desire to get beyond mere notional religion, and to lay a living hold on living truth. And the way to do this is to take our common thoughts of right and wrong into the light of God, and connect them with Him, and act them out in the conviction that they come straight from Him. One of the first results of such an effort to act up to conscience will be the conviction that there is in us something essentially wrong inwardly, which of ourselves we are quite unable to set right, — that to do this is a task to which our own internal resources are wholly inadequate. And the more honestly the attempt is made, the more entirely will a man feel that the powers of restoration he needs must lie out of himself, above himself. Of such powers no tidings reach him from any quarter of the universe, save only from the Revelation that is in Christ.[1]

If, then, this prime essential condition of all spiritual progress be present, namely, an awakened conscience, there are various means by which the life begun can be fed and nourished. Here again I must repeat that I am unwilling to trespass on the duty of the Christian minister, but I trust you will bear with me, if I briefly mention a few things which perhaps you do not usually associate with college instruction. For otherwise I should not be able to speak the truth on this matter, and I believe that the reality of the things of religion suffers greatly from their being confined solely to the church and pulpits, and being considered unseasonable and out of taste if even alluded to by laymen and at other times.

1. The first means, then, of spiritual growth is Prayer; not the repeating of forms merely, nor the saying of words, but the honest, sincere, often voiceless prayer, which comes into real contact, heart to heart, with Him to whom we pray. To pray thus is not the easy thing we are sometimes apt to imagine. It is not learned in a day, but is the

[1] Note VII.

result of many an earnest, devout effort. It requires the whole being to concur, — the understanding, the emotions, the will, the spirit. It is an energy of the total soul, far beyond any mere intellectual act. But to the spiritual life it is as absolutely essential as inbreathing of fresh air is to the lungs and the bodily life.

2. Then there is Meditation, — the quiet, serious, devout fixing of the mind, from time to time, on some great truth or fact of religion, holding it before the mind steadily, silently brooding over it till it becomes warm and vital, and melts into us. This habit of devout meditation is recommended, by good men who have practiced it, as eminently useful. But it is not much in keeping with the tone of the present day. For with all our pretensions to enlightenment, are we not now a talking, desultory, rather than a meditative generation? Whatever other mental acquirements we may possess, we are certainly not rich in

> "The harvest of the quiet eye,
> That sleeps and broods on its own heart."

And yet, without something of this meditative habit, it is impossible to lay living hold of the first truths of morality and religion.

It were well, therefore, if we should betimes turn aside from life's bustle, and "impose a sabbath" on our too busy spirits, that the things of sense, being for a while shut out, the unseen things may come into us with power.

3. Again, few things are more helpful than the study of the lives of the most eminent Christians from the beginning. The Roman Church has her lives of the saints, some of them of doubtful authenticity. The Universal Church should have a catena of lives of the best men of each age, from primitive times till now. It would include the saintly spirits of all ages, from all countries, men of all ranks, of every variety of temper, taken from the most diverse churches. Such a catena would be the strongest of all external evidences. It would exhibit Christianity, not so much as a system of doctrines, but as a power of life, adequate to subdue the strongest wills, to renew the darkest hearts, to leaven the most opposite characters. If an intimate study of it were more common, how much would it do to heal divisions, to deepen and enlarge the sympathies of all Christians, by the exhibition of their common spiritual ancestry!

4. But if such an intimacy with good men gone is beneficial, not less so is intercourse with the living, our elders, or companions more advanced than ourselves. They will understand what I mean, who have ever known any one in whom the power of Christian love has had its perfect work. As from time to time they turned to these, did they not find, from the irregularities of their own minds, and the distractions of the world, shelter and a soothing calm? "The constant transpiration" of their characters came home with an evidence more direct, more intimate, more persuasive than any other. "Whatever is right, whatever is wrong, in this perplexing world," one thing they felt must be right: to live as these lived, to be of the spirit they were of. Impressions of this kind affect us more powerfully in youth than in later years, yet they are not denied us even in mature manhood. Happy are those who have known some such friends. They are not confined to any age or station, but may be found among poor men and unlearned, as readily as among the most gifted. Let us cherish the society of such persons while we may, and the remembrance of them when that intercourse is over. For we may

be quite sure of this, that life has nothing else to give more pure, more precious, than such companionship.

5. But the last, and by far the most powerful, of all outward aids to spiritual growth, is to bring the heart and spirit into close contact with that Life which is portrayed by the four Evangelists. But before we can do this satisfactorily, some may say, we must settle a host of difficult problems, fight out our way through a whole jungle of vexed and intricate questions. "One knows the interminable discussions of modern criticisms on the origin, the authenticity, and the mutual relations of the four Gospels. But for our present purpose we can leave all these questions on one side. The authenticity of the evangelistic teaching will always prove itself better by its own nature and self-evidencing power, than by any criticism of the documents." To say this is not to disparage criticism, which has its own place and use. But that place is not the central or vital one. Criticism is not religion, and by no process can it be substituted for it. It is not the critic's eye, but the child's heart, that most truly discerns the countenance that looks out from the pages of the Gospels. If we would not miss or distort

that image, let us come to it with an open heart, feeling our need of help. Such a way of studying the Gospels, simple, open-hearted, reverent, is the truest, healthiest, most penetrating means of feeding the divine life. When once by long, single-hearted, steadfast contemplation the impression has graven itself within, it is the strongest, it is the most indelible that we know. Dogmatic convictions may change, criticism may shift its ground, but that image will abide, rooted in the deepest seats of moral life. Whatever storms may shake us in a troubled time, this anchor, if any, will "hold." Try before all things, especially while you are young and open to impressions, to bring understanding, imagination, heart, conscience, under the power of that master vision. That image, or rather that Person, so human, yet so entirely divine, has a power to fill the imagination, to arrest the affections, to deepen and purify the conscience, which nothing else in the world has. No end so worthy of your literary and philosophic training here, as to enable you to do this more firmly and intelligently. All criticism which tends to make the lineaments of that countenance shine out more impressively shall be welcome. Whatever tends to dim it, or remove it to a distance, we shall disregard. For we know with a certainty which far transcends any certainty of criticism, that He is true.

But if we would deepen and perpetuate in ourselves the impressions thus made, we must remember that the surest way is to act on them. There is, I fear, a tendency in all of us to desire clear convictions and vivid feelings about these things, and to rest there, content with convictions and feelings. And so they come to naught. If they are not to be merely head notions or evanescent feelings, they must be taken into the will, and pass out into our actions. This is what our Lord said: If any man will do His will, he shall know of the doctrine whether it be of God. Knowledge is to follow doing, not precede it. In order to understand, we must commence by putting into practice what we already know. "Unfortunately all ages and parties have gone to work the other way, adjourning the doing of the doctrine, hastening to busy themselves with the theory of it." And each individual man must be aware of this tendency in himself, the desire for a fully mapped-out system of truth, which, after he has got it, he will begin to think of practicing. But we shall never get it thus. To do what we know to be right first, however little that may be, to follow out the light we have, this is the only way to get more light. Whatever good thoughts or feelings we have, we must try earnestly to embody them in act, if we wish to grow. But to will and do is so much harder than to speak and speculate, and even feel. This is the reason we turn aside from the former, and give ourselves so much to the latter. But it is in vain we do so. In spiritual things there is no road to higher light without obedience to conscience. This gives solidity to a man's character, and assurance to his faith, as nothing else does.

I have dwelt on this, the spiritual side of our subject, at what may seem disproportionate length. But I have done so from the belief that it is an aspect of truth which at present is being too much disregarded by the most ardent Culturists, and by some also of the strongest advocates of general education. And so by losing sight of it, or willfully rejecting it, not only is the whole economy of the human spirit deranged, but even the purely intellectual faculties and powers are deprived of their highest objects. Even among those who do not take the entirely secular view of life, and shut out religion altogether, there seems to be a tendency to expect religion to come as the last result of a large and laborious culture, — that, in short, we may end with it, but are not to begin it, — that we must first learn all that science can teach us of the outer world of nature, then all that philosophy can teach us of the the inner world of man, then all that history, and the philosophy of history, can teach us of the progress of the race, and then, as the last consummation, as the copestone on this great edifice of knowledge, theology may possibly be built. And when the true theology has got itself achieved, there may come religion; that is, we may proceed to believe and act on it. I do not say that this view is put forth in so many words, but it seems to be latent in many minds, and implied as a first principle in much that is said in the present time. Not, of course, by the multitude, — it is not among them that such a view would prevail, — but it is entertained by many of those who are reputed "advanced thinkers," as the phrase goes, and from them it filters down to the platforms and the newspapers, and helps to swell that most wearisome chorus of self-laudation which is evermore rising up about this most wonderful and enlightened age. Instead, however, of coming as the last consummation, I believe it will be found that, in far the greatest number of men who ever become really religious, the sense of God is awakened early, a germ of life growing and expanding from childhood, round which learning and culture gathered afterwards. This I believe to be the natural, and by far the most frequent, history of the best men. If, on the other hand, we postpone spiritual things till we have completed, or even far advanced, our investigations, there is great danger that they will never come at all. I do not say that some men, a very few, may not have awakened to the practical sense of God late in life, and only after long wanderings in the world of thought without Him. God has many ways of bringing men's spirits to Himself, and we dare not venture to say He shall lead any man in this way and not in that. Only this we can say, that for men to arrive at divine truth as the last stage in a long process of culture and investigation, is not His usual way of leading men, and that when it does take place it comes not in the way of gradual sequence, not as it were the last step in a long induction. Not as a natural sequence, but rather as a convulsion, will such revelation be likely to come, with a confession of failure, with a rending of old habits of thought and of godless associations, with the acknowledgment that much of life has been wasted, and that the chief thing Culture has taught is that not in itself is God to be found.

Speculation, we may believe, "reaches its final rest and home in faith," but the faith has generally been present in the heart before the speculation began, and has accompanied it more or less consciously through all its travellings. Where the faith has only appeared in the end, it will be because speculation has acknowledged itself unable livingly to lay hold on God, and has resigned the searcher over to another higher than itself.

The practical upshot of all I have said is this: Do not let us adjourn being religious till we have become learned. It may be to some a tempting, but it is a dangerous experiment. If we wish really to be good, and to know the good, we should begin early, begin at once.

I may have dwelt too long on this. But it

is because I see so strong a tendency abroad to begin at the wrong end, to deal first and prominently with the intellectual side of things, and to expect all good from that, that I feel constrained to urge on all who hear me, especially on the young, to avoid this, to begin as well as to end with God revealed in Christ, and communion with Him. So shall they have their whole natures grounded, established, braced for the stern siftings which in this age assuredly await us.

It is high time now to ask how Culture and Religion act and react on each other. Side glances have been taken at this subject throughout these lectures. To give a full and systematic view of all their relations I have not proposed, even if I had the power. A few words, however, must be said.

If, as we saw, Religion, or the impulse in man to seek God, and Culture, or the impulse in man to seek his own highest perfection, both come from the same Divine source, it is clear that as they are in themselves — that is, as God sees them — there can be no opposition, there must be perfect harmony between them. Both together, they must be working towards that full revelation of

God and that good of man towards which we believe creation moves. But as soon as we regard them not absolutely, but as man has made them, that is, as they have appeared in history, immediately we find that they have not always conspired harmoniously towards one great end, that for long periods they have moved on separate lines, that sometimes they have come into actual collision. And the reason of this is obvious. Few men can take in more than one point of view at a time, none can habitually embrace and maintain a universal and absolute view of things. And so it has come to pass that these two powers, as they start from different centres, have continued each to work on under the impulse of the leading idea which gave it birth, without taking much account of the idea which animated the other. Culture, with its eye fixed on man's perfection, has been busy with the means that tend towards this, that is appropriating the large results which human effort, thought, and experience have gathered from past centuries. Religion, on the other hand, starting, not from the view of man's perfection, but of God's existence, in the consciousness of this, however dim and unenlightened, has been entirely absorbed in the results that flow out of this relation, — the sense of dependence, the duty of obedience and self-surrender, and man's total inability to meet this claim. And in its absorption it has, for light, looked — inward, to the monitions, however obscure, of conscience; outward, to whatever aid nature and history supply; upward, to that light, higher than nature, which has come direct from heaven. And thus each, self-enwrapt, has taken little account of its neighbor.

But if these two forces are to cease from their isolation, and combine, as we may hope, towards some better result than the world has yet seen, the question arises, Are they to work as two coördinate and equipollent powers, or is one to be subordinate to the other, and if so, which? To this question the old answer is still, we feel, the true one. To Religion belongs of right the sovereign place, and this because it is a more direct emanation from the Divine source; it finds its response in the deeper places of our being; it is the earlier manifestation in the history of the race; the earlier in the life of the individual, and it will be the last. But though its place is primary, it cannot be independent of thought and knowledge; nay, the religion of each age must, in a large measure, be conditioned by the state of knowledge existing in that age. We see this in the past history of religion, and we see how fruitless, I should rather say how disastrous, have been the effects, when religion has tried to close itself against the rising tide of knowledge. And the lesson which the past teaches, religious men would do well to learn, and keep an open side to the influx of all the new knowledge which each age achieves, to appropriate this, and absorb it into their religious convictions. So far from being jealous or suspicious of ascertained scientific truths, or even indifferent to them, they should feel that such prejudices are wrong, that they are bound to welcome all such truths, being sure that, in as far as they are truths, God means them to be known, and wills them to be incorporated into our thoughts of Him and of His ways.

And here I cannot better express my own thought than by quoting words which Bishop Temple lately spoke on this subject. "I have," he said, in a public address delivered in his own diocese, "a real conviction that all this study of science, rightly pursued, comes from the providence of God; that it is in accordance with His will that we should study His works, and that as He has given us a spiritual revelation in His Word, so also has He given us a natural revelation in His creation. I am convinced that there is nothing to lose, but everything to gain, by a true and careful study of God's works; that the more light we can get, the more cultivation of our understanding, and the more thorough discipline of our intellect by the study of all this which God has scattered in such wonderful profusion around us, so much the better shall we be able not only to serve Him in our vocation, but to understand the meaning of His spiritual revelations. I am convinced that all light of whatever kind is good, and comes from God; that all knowledge comes from Him, and can be used in His service; that nothing which really adds to the knowledge of the world is for a moment to be despised; that, on the contrary, it should be the effort of all who undertake to instruct their brethren in religious truth, to show that we feel that religious truth and secular truth are not only capable of being reconciled, but really come from the same God who is the God of all truth. Therefore, so far from desiring that there should be divorce between these two, I should wish, on the contrary, that every effort should be made by all who are concerned in religious teaching, to pervade the study of science with their own religious feeling; to study science with the constant recollection of that God whose works are the subject of science; to study science with minds perpetually uplifted towards Him who is the author both of order and of beauty; to study the laws of nature with a perpetual recollection of Him who ordained them. I know that it is not only possible, but that both science and religion will gain by the union."

The truth enforced in these words is so obvious that hardly any one will think of directly denying it, however little many may be ready to act on it. One thing, however, I would have you observe, that they presuppose the thought of God taken into science, and not first found there. It may be well to dwell a little on this, and to illustrate these general views somewhat more in detail. For, stated generally, the truth above expressed may sound like a truism. It is only when we come to particular points that the difficulties really begin.

It lies, we know, at the root of all religion, to believe that this system of things is really from God, that the Divine thought presided at its origin, and that the same is present upholding and carrying forward this beautiful order with which we are now encompassed. Any so-called conclusions of science which deny this, and suggest another origin of the world than the will and thought of God, religion must reject as subversive of its first principle. But, this granted, religion must leave it to science to discover what is the method which the Divine thought has followed, what have been the processes by which it has evolved the order we now behold. All facts really established by science religion must receive, nay, more, ought to welcome, and incorporate into its own view of the universe, allowing them to modify that view in as far as this may be necessary. In refusing to do this, in looking with suspicion, if not with positive hostility, on the fresh discoveries of each age, religious persons, since the days of Galileo downwards, have often erred, and given just grounds for complaint to the advocates of science. On the other hand, it must be said that scientific, or rather quasi-scientific, persons have sometimes been hasty to thrust on religion for acceptance a number of crude hypotheses, as if they were scientific verities. For the solid body of science seems to throw out before it a pretentious penumbra of hypotheses and presuppositions, which often, in the name of science, call on religion to surrender at discretion. It is not, however, the really scientific, the original discoverers, who for the most part deal in these. Such men dwell in the solid body of science, and are careful not to stray beyond it. The penumbra I speak of is mainly tenanted by another sort, — persons of small scientific capacity, but of busy minds, greedy of novelties, and rapid to extemporize big philosophies out of the materials which science furnishes. From such comes the assertion, often heard nowadays, that miracle is impossible. This, however, though urged in the name of science, is no scientific truth at all. It is only a large and pretentious generalization, bred no doubt out of the scientific atmosphere which more or less envelops even popular thought, but wholly unwarranted by genuine science. When religion is called on to accept this nostrum of the destructive critics, it is not prejudice or narrowness, but truth, that compels her to meet it with a direct denial. Such an assertion has nothing to support it but *a priori* assumption; it is not warranted by anything we know, and is foreign to the moderation of true science. Nothing that has been ascertained by physical inquiry, nothing that mental philosophy has made good, would justify such dogmatism. It implies the possession of a much wider, more entire knowledge of the universe than any yet attained, or perhaps that will be attained in our present state. Religion, therefore, is at one with sound philosophy in refusing to admit such an assumption. And this quite apart from that other consideration, that if true it would relegate to the region of myth one half of the Gospel histories, and render the other half of no authority if it were imbedded in such a mass of fable. The statement, then, that miracles are in themselves impossible, being a wholly groundless assumption, the question of their actual occurrence becomes one of purely historical evidence. What that evidence is has been often stated, and will be restated from time to time according as the shifting views of each age require. But perhaps men's belief in that evidence can never be determined entirely on objective grounds. The strength of the evidence will always be differently estimated by different minds, but owing to other considerations, and especially according as they have a latent belief or disbelief in their possibility and likelihood.

Again, when we are told that to the modern scientific sense the idea of God the Father resolves itself into that of "the universal order," or into "that stream of tendency by which all things strive to fulfill the law of their being," how is religion to deal with this assertion? Or again, when instead of Christ we are offered as the modern equivalent "an absent and unseen power of goodness?" It is not resistance to modern intelligence, but defense of the very "core" of spiritual life, that makes religion withstand such intrusions of so-called science or criticism into her own inmost recesses. Once again we must repeat, the things of the Spirit are truly apprehended only by the spirit and the conscience of man. If God is known then only truly when the heart communes with Him, substitutes for religious entities which would make such communion impossible are by this very fact disproved. Those abstractions which criticism and philosophy, divorced from the Spirit, offer, are but pale and lifeless shadows. The things of revelation, the truths which St. John and St. Paul lived by, and all Christian men since have tried to live by, when pared down by these modern processes, are extinct. No doubt science and philosophy have something to do with shaping the intellectual forms in which spiritual truths shall be expressed. But when criticism pretends to penetrate into the inner essence of spiritual truths, and to supply us with modern equivalents for them, it is then time to remind it that it is overstepping the limits which are proper to it. For it is to the spirit and conscience of men that spiritual truth makes its appeal, and by these in the last resort it must be apprehended. It will be said, I know, How are we to ascertain what really are those realities to which the conscience and the spirit of men witness, seeing that with regard to these men are so divided?

I am aware of the difficulty. Yet we cannot in deference to it recede from the first principle, that spiritual things are to be spiritually discerned; that the coming home of a religious truth to the spirit of a man, and fitting into it, is to that man the highest evidence of its truth, and that this is the thing we should each seek first. He who has felt the self-evidencing power of truth will know this to be its best proof. Where this is not present, intellectual arguments will do little, as these may be adduced equally on that side or on this. It may be that we have felt little of this evidencing power of truth, — that there are few truths which have so come home to us. But all men have felt some measure of it. They have at least their sense of right and wrong in its more obvious bearings. Whoso shall try to live and act on this, so using the small light he has, he shall receive more.

If it still be urged, Such inward conviction is at best personal to the individual who has it, we wish for some test of religious truth which shall be impersonal and universal; it may be replied, that while the highest evidence in the things of religion must necessarily rest on personal grounds, there are other tests more general, though of a secondary and subordinate kind as far as cogency is concerned. Some such outward test may be found by observing what are those religious truths which the best, most spiritually-minded men of all ages have chiefly laid to heart. As

Aristotle found a clew towards a moral standard by taking the general suffrage of the morally wisest men, so may we do in some measure with regard to spiritual things. Still, though this may help us somewhat, in the last resort we must fall back on the truth that light is self-evidencing, — as light natural, so light spiritual. Seeing, feeling is believing, and the conviction thus produced must be an inward and personal thing, not readily nor adequately represented in the language of the intellect. To adopt the words of a profound thinker, whom I have already quoted in these lectures, "An intellectual form our spiritual apprehensions must receive, that the demand of our intellectual nature may be met. But still that which is spiritual must be spiritually discerned, and I would not seek to recommend the doctrine of the atonement by what might be called bringing it down to the level of the understanding. I seek rather to raise the understanding to that which is above it, and to that exercise of thought on spiritual things in which we feel ourselves brought near to what is divine and infinite, and made partakers in the knowledge of the love which passeth knowledge."

Or in the words of another great living teacher, belonging to a different school: — "The inward witness to the truth lodged in our hearts is a match for the most learned infidel or sceptic that ever lived. In spiritual things, the most acute of reasoners and most profound of thinkers, the most instructed in earthly knowledge, is nothing except he has also within him the presence of the Spirit of truth. Human knowledge, though of great power when joined to a pure and humble faith, is of no power when opposed to it." I am aware that words like these, the "inward witness," "the witness of God's Spirit with man's spirit," may be used as catch-words in a way that makes them meaningless. But to this abuse they are liable only in common with all words expressive of high and spiritual things. When two such men as Dr. M'Leod Campbell and Dr. Newman, so differently trained, and with views so opposed in many things, combine to speak of "the witness of the Spirit," and to urge men to seek it, we may be quite sure that it is not any mere hearsay they are repeating, but that they are speaking of somewhich they know and feel to be a reality.

Before passing entirely from this subject

let me ask, Have faith and worship to do with the known or with the unknown? It is sometimes said that faith and worship only begin where knowledge ends. At other times we hear the exact contrary asserted, — that we cannot believe any truth or worship any being of which we have not complete understanding, that in fact the circle of definite knowledge and of possible faith are coextensive. These assertions seem both equally wide of the truth. It is in knowledge that faith and worship begin. We believe in God, and we worship God because of that which He has made known to us of Himself, in conscience first, and then more fully in revelation. Indeed, the very simplest acceptance of the truths of conscience, and the obeying of them, instead of choosing the pleasures of sense, is essentially of the nature of faith. And the knowledge thus brought home to the spirit, it feels to be positive knowledge, — a circle of light in which it dwells. True it is that what is thus known reaches out on all sides to what is unknown, — the light is on all sides encompassed with darkness. But the existence of the surrounding darkness does not make the light, such as it is, to be less light. And the faith and worship do not confine themselves within the region of light, but pass out into the outer circle, — go on from the known to the unknown. But in this they are doing no violence to reason; nay, they are fulfilling the behest of the highest reason, which feels instinctively that while there is something of God which is within our ken, there must be much more which stretches beyond it. At the same time it feels equally assured that what lies beyond our present, perhaps even our future, vision, will never contradict that which is within it — that the true knowledge which the conscience and spirit now have will never be put to shame.[1]

But while these two elements, the known and the unknown, coexist, and we believe always will coexist, in faith and worship, the relation in which the two elements stand to each other must undergo some change with the widening of human knowledge and experience. The moral conceptions of the race have been, in the course of ages, not radically changed, but expanded, deepened, purified by many agencies. Our moral and religious ideas are not unaffected even by discoveries in regions which at first sight might seem most remote from them.

[1] Note VIII.

The view of the universe as science leads us to conceive it must react on our thoughts of God. Opening out before us the vast scale on which He works, and acquainting us with some of the methods of His working, it counteracts the limitations which are apt to arise from the human forms under which we think of Him. These forms are necessary and true. It is only because man has in himself some image of God that he can think of Him at all. But round this true conception, so formed, there are apt to gather accretions from man's weakness and imperfection, to which the expansive views of science furnish a wholesome antidote. Again, do men's views of morality, as time goes on, get more deep, more just and humane? And to this result nothing, I believe, has so much contributed as eighteen centuries of Christianity, notwithstanding all the corruptions it has undergone. Then this improved moral perception, from whatever sources derived, reacts directly on religious belief, by removing obstructions that hide from us true views of God, and enabling us to think of Him more nearly as He is. As our conception of what true righteousness consists in improves, so must our thought of Him who is the Righteous One. Idolatry has been said to be the preferring of an image of God which we feel to be imperfect, but which has adapted and contracted itself to our weakness, instead of pressing on to the most perfect image attainable, in the light and heat of which our imperfections may be exposed and burned up. In short, it is the retaining between our hearts and God an imperfect image of Him, when it is in our power to attain to a truer and more perfect vision. Every increase of knowledge, whether gathered from history, or from the world without, or from the world within, may be a help towards forming a better conception of God's nature and of His ways, and ought to be so used. If we refuse either to increase our knowledge that we may so use it, or neglect to turn it when increased to this its highest purpose, and so are content to rest in less worthy thoughts of the Divine character, can we then excuse ourselves from the sin of idolatry? One who really has confidence in truth — truth alike of science, of philosophy, of history, and of faith — will desire to see truth sought and advanced along all the diverse lines on which it is to be found. He may not see the point at which all these lines converge, but he has perfect faith that they do converge, whether he sees it or not. He can be satisfied with seeing but a little for a time, assured that he will yet see that little open on a fuller day. Believe in God, and bid all knowledge speed. Sooner or later the full harmony will reveal itself, the discords and contradictions disappear.

Before closing this whole subject let me again repeat, what has been more than once hinted already, that Culture, when it will not accept its proper place as secondary, but sets up to be the guiding principle of life, forfeits that which might be its highest charm. Indeed, even when it does not professedly turn its back on faith, yet if it claims to be paramount, it will generally be found that it has cultivated every other side of man's nature but the devout one. There is no more forlorn sight than that of a man highly gifted, elaborately cultivated, with all the other capacities of his nature strong and active, but those of faith and reverence dormant. And this, be it said, is the pattern of man in which Culture, made the chief good, would most likely issue. On the other hand, when it assumes its proper place, illumined by faith, and animated by devout aspiration, it acquires a dignity and depth which of itself it cannot attain. From faith it receives its highest and most worthy objects. It is chastened and purified from self-reference and conceit. It is prized no longer merely for its own sake, or because it exalts the possessor of it, but because it enables him to be of use to others who have been less fortunate. In a word, it ceases to be self-isolated, and seeks to communicate itself as widely as it may. So Culture is transmuted from an intellectual attainment into a spiritual grace. This seems the light in which all who are admitted to a higher cultivation should learn to regard their endowments, whatever they be. Why is a small moiety, with no peculiar claim on society, so highly favored, taken for a while from the dust and pressure of the world, and set apart in calm retreats like these, that here they may have access to the best learning of the time? Not certainly that we should waste these precious hours in sloth, neither that we should merely make our bread by learning; not that we should seek and enjoy it as a selfish luxury, and, piquing ourselves on the enlightenment and refinement it brings, look down with disdain on the illiterate crowd; but that, when we have been cultivated ourselves, we should go into the world and do what we can to impart to others whatever good thing we ourselves have received. There is a temptation incident to the studious to seclude themselves from others, and lose themselves in their own thoughts and books. But we must try to resist this, and remember that since we have freely received, we are bound freely to give. This it is which makes Culture a really honorable and beneficent power.

But there is a point of view from which this whole subject may be regarded, and I cannot close these lectures without alluding to it. There is a higher vantage-ground, seen from which all these balancings between Culture and Religion, man's effort and God's working, would disappear, and all relations would at once fall into their right place. If there is reason to believe that God Himself is the great educator, and that His purpose, in all His dealings with men, is to educate them for Himself, what a new light would be thrown on all the ground over which we have travelled! This is not the place to enter into an examination of the statements of Scripture which may bear on this subject.

This only may be said, the belief that it is God's purpose to bring man out of the darkness of his evil and ignorance into the light of His own righteousness and love, seems every way consistent with what we know of His character as revealed in Christ. It is in harmony with the whole tenor of His life and teaching who said, "I, if I be lifted up from the earth, will draw all men unto myself." In this purpose there is a door of hope opened for all humanity.

But then comes the thought that, though the door is opened, all do not enter by it. Multitudes never know that such a door exists; many more know, and pass it by. That this should be God's purpose and yet that men should have the power to resist this purpose, to close their wills against it, this, next to the existence of evil at all, is the greatest of all mysteries. I have no wish, indeed it is of no use, to try to conceal it; it is a dark outstanding fact which must strike every one. If it is the Divine purpose to educate man, it is but too evident that a great multitude, perhaps the majority of men, leave this earth without, as far as we can see, the rudiments of the Divine education being even begun in them. Not to think of their case is impossible for any man, and the more generous and sympathetic any one is, the more heavily will it weigh on him. It must be owned that there are times when this thought becomes to those who dwell on it very overpowering. There are some in whom it seems to "stagger" all their powers of faith. Scripture offers no solution of this great perplexity, reason is helpless before it, human systems, in trying to explain it, only make it worse. What, then, are we to do? We can but fall back on that ancient word of faith, "Shall not the Judge of all the earth do right?" We must leave it to God Himself to solve, — assured that in the end He will solve it perfectly, will supremely justify Himself.

Still, notwithstanding all that to us seems like failure, the belief in this purpose of God to train for Himself all who will, is, if we can but apprehend it, a thought full of strength and comfort. It is not only the highest hope, but the only real hope for humanity that exists. It embraces everything that is good in the Culture theory, and how much more! If Culture were what Culturists announce it to be, the one hope for men, what a very moiety of the race are they to whom it is open! A few prepared for it in youth, with health, leisure, some resources, have access to it. But what of all the others, even if the brightest dreams of educationists and advanced politicians were to be fulfilled? The hope that is in Christianity, far short as the accomplishment has hitherto fallen of the ideal, is still in its very nature a hope for all, and it does actually reach multitudes whom Culture must leave out. How many are the occurrences of life which Culture can make nothing of, which it must abandon in dispair? There are a thousand circumstances, I might say the larger portion of the stuff life is made of, out of which Culture can extract nothing. What has it to say to "poverty, destitution, and oppression, to pain and suffering, diseases long and violent, all that is frightful and revolting?" What word can it speak to the heart-weary and desponding, those for whom life has been a failure, who have no more hope here? But it is just where mere Culture is powerless that the faith that One higher than ourselves is training us, comes in most consolingly. Those untoward things, of which human effort can make nothing, failure, disappointment, sickness, have often ere now been felt by sufferers to be parts of the discipline by which He was training them for Himself. And this faith has many a time had power to lighten, sometimes it has even irradiated, things which else would have been insupportable. To adapt the words of Wordsworth to a purpose not alien to their own, — in faith a power abides which can feed

> "A calm, a beautiful, and silent fire,
> From the incumbrances of mortal life,
> From error, disappointment, — nay, from guilt;
> And sometimes, so relenting justice wills,
> From palpable oppressions of despair."

It is a "many-chambered" school, that in which God trains. None are excluded from it, all are welcome. It has room for all gifts, all circumstances, all conditions. It makes allowance for defects and shortcomings which are ruin in this world. Trained in this school many have reached a high place, who have had no "tincture of letters." Most of us must have known some, especially in the humbler places of society, who had not any of this world's learning, had never heard even the names of the greatest poets and philosophers, yet who, without help from these, had been led, by some secret way, up to the serenest, most beautiful heights of character. It is indeed a many-chambered school.

These were led through some of its chambers to their end, we are being led through others. To those who, like ourselves, have large opportunities of Culture placed within their reach, these are the instruments of the divine discipline. It is part of that discipline to put large opportunities in men's hands, and to leave it to themselves whether they will use or neglect them. There shall be no coercion to make us turn them to account. Occasions of learning and self-improvement come, stay with us for a while, then pass. And the wheels of time shall not be reversed to bring them back, once they are gone. If we neglect them, we shall be permanent losers for this life. We cannot say how much we may be losers hereafter. But if we do what we can to use them while they are granted, we shall have learnt one lesson of the heavenly discipline, and shall be the better prepared for the others, whether of action or endurance, which are yet to come.

This view of our life as a process of education, which God seeks to carry on in each man, is not, it may be granted, the view of God and of His dealings with us which suggests itself when men first begin to think seriously. Neither is it one which it is easy to hold steadily amid all the distractions of time, or to defend against all objections that may be urged from the anomalies that surround us. But I think it is one which will more commend itself as people advance. It will approve itself as setting forth an end which seems altogether worthy of Him who made us.

And now I have come round to one of the leading thoughts with which I set out. Those who heard my first lecture may remember that it was stated as the end of Culture to set before the young a high and worthy aim or ideal of life, and to train in them the powers necessary to attain it. It was further stated that while each man should have in view an ideal which he should strive to reach, what that ideal should be is to be determined for each man by the natural gifts he is endowed with, and by the circumstances in which he finds himself placed. That end of Culture was then stated, and we passed on. But now I think the belief in a divine education open to each man and to all men, takes up into itself all that is true in the end proposed by Culture, supplements and perfects it. It is right that we should have an aim of our own, with something peculiar in it, determined by our individuality and our surroundings; but this may readily degenerate into exclusive narrowness, unless it has for a background the great thought, that there is a kingdom of God within us, around us, and above us, in which we, with all our powers and aims, are called to be conscious workers. Towards the forwarding of this silent, ever-advancing kingdom, our little work, whatever it be, if good and true, may contribute something. And this thought lends to any calling, however lowly, a consecration which is wanting even to the loftiest self-chosen ideals. But even if our aim should be frustrated and our work come to naught, yet the failure of our most cherished plans may be more than compensated. In the thought that we are members of this kingdom, already begun, here and now, yet reaching forward through all time, we shall have a reserve of consolation better than any which success without this could give. When we are young, if we are of an aspiring nature, we are apt to make much of our ideals, and to fancy that in them we shall find a good not open to the vulgar. And then that universal kingdom, which embraces in itself all true ideals, is, if not wholly disbelieved, yet thought of as remote. But as life goes on, the ideals we set before us, even if attained, dwindle in importance, and that kingdom grows. We come to feel that it is indeed the substance, those the shadows. Were it not well, then, to begin with the substance, to learn to apprehend the reality of that kingdom which is all around us now, whether we recognize it or not, — to take our aims and endeavors into it, that they may be made part of it, however small, — to surrender ourselves to it, that our lives may do something towards its advancement, and that so we may become fellow-workers, however humble, with all the wise and good who have gone before us, and with Him who made them what they were? Only they who early thus begin

> "Through the world's long day of strife
> Still chant their morning song."

APPENDIX.

Note I. — Page 24.

The following passages from Fichte's *Lectures on the Nature of a Scholar* (translation) illustrate the moral and religious root which underlies all true culture. Though these Lectures were meant to be popular, they are still colored by the language of the author's philosophic system. By the "Divine Idea," especially, Fichte seems to have meant, not, as we might suppose, our ideas about God, but rather what we should express by the words the Divine Nature, or even God: —

"In every age, the kind of education and spiritual culture, by means of which the age hopes to lead mankind to the knowledge of the ascertained part of the Divine Idea, is the learned culture of the age; and every man who partakes in this culture is the scholar of the age. . . . The whole of the training and culture, which an age calls learned education, is only a means towards a knowledge of the attainable portion of the Divine Idea, and is only valuable in so far as it actually is such a means, and truly fulfills its purpose." . . .

"He only shall be esteemed as a scholar who, through the learned culture of his age, has actually attained a knowledge of the Idea, or at least strives with life and strength to attain it. Through the learned culture of his age, I say; for, if a man without the use of this means, can arrive at a knowledge of the Idea by some other means, (and I am far from denying that he may do so), yet such an one will be unable either to communicate his knowledge theoretically, or to realize it immediately in the world according to any well-defined rule, because he must want that knowledge of his age, and of the means of operating upon it, which can only be acquired in schools of learning."

Again, "Either the scholar has actually laid hold of the Divine Idea, in so far as it is attainable by man, or of a particular part of it, — has actually laid hold of it, and penetrated into its significance, until it stands lucid and distinct before him, so that it has become his own possession, an element in his personality; and then he is a complete and finished scholar, a man who has gone through his studies: Or he as yet only strives and struggles to attain a clear insight into the Idea generally, or into a particular portion of it, from which he, for his part, will penetrate the whole: — already, one by one, sparks of light arise on every side, and disclose a higher world before him; but they do not yet unite into one indivisible whole, — they vanish, as they came, without his bidding, and he cannot yet bring them under the dominion of his will; — and then he is a progressive, a self-forming scholar, — a student. That it be really the Idea which is either possessed or struggled after is common to both of these; if the striving is only after the outward form, the mere letter of learned culture then we have; if the round is finished, the complete, if it is unfinished, the progressive *Bungler.*"

Again, "Man is not placed in the world of sense alone, but the essential root of his being is, as we have seen, in God. Hurried along by sense and its impulses, the consciousness of this Life in God may be readily hidden from him; and then, however noble may be his nature, he lives in strife and disunion with himself; in discord and unhappiness, without true dignity and enjoyment of life. But when the consciousness of the true source of his existence first rises upon him, and he joyfully resigns himself to it, till his being is steeped in the thought, then peace and joy and blessedness flow in upon his soul. And it lies in the Divine Idea that all men must come to this gladdening consciousness, — that the outward and tasteless Finite Life may be pervaded by the Infinite, and so enjoyed; and to this end, all who have been filled with the Divine Idea have labored and shall still labor, that this consciousness, in its purest possible form, may be spread throughout the race."

This language is not exactly that of Christian theology, but it is nearer to the kingdom of heaven than most utterances of British philosophy.

Note II. — Page 34.

This passage occurs in *The Freeness of the Gospel*, by the late Thomas Erskine of Linlathen. When the first of these lectures was delivered, he was yet alive. Before the closing one was given he had breathed his last, on Sunday, the 20th March, 1870. *The Freeness of the Gospel* was first published nearly fifty years ago. For long the author had abstained from republishing this or any of those other works which so deeply touched the minds of many in Scotland during the last generation. But in his latter days he had allowed a new edition of the work, from which this quotation is made, to be prepared by a friend and even himself dictated some corrections. This edition has appeared since the death of the revered author.

NOTE III. — Page 36.

FOR some of the thoughts here expressed on the influence of Greece, I am indebted to the first of Dr. Newman's *Lectures on University Subjects*. Especially in what I have said of Homer, I have ventured to adopt not only Dr. Newman's thought, but also some of his expressions. The passage in the original lecture is so graceful, and puts an old subject in so new a light, that it is here given more at length.

"In the country which has been the fountain-head of intellectual gifts, in the age which preceded or introduced the first formations of Human Society; in an era scarcely historical, we may dimly discern an almost mythical personage, who, putting out of consideration the actors in Old Testament history, may be called the first Apostle of Civilization. Like an Apostle in another order of things, he was poor and a wanderer, and feeble in the flesh, though he was to do such great things, and to live in the mouths of a hundred generations, and a thousand tribes. A blind old man whose wanderings were such that, when he became famous, his birthplace could not be ascertained.

> "Seven famous towns contend for Homer dead,
> Through which the living Homer begged his bread."

Yet he had a name in his day, and, little guessing in what vast measures his wish would be answered, he supplicated with a tender human feeling, as he wandered over the islands of the Ægean and the Asian coasts, that those who had known and loved him would cherish his memory when he was absent. Unlike the proud boast of the Roman poet, if he spoke it in earnest, 'Exegi monumentum ære perennius,' he did but indulge the hope that one whose coming had been expected with pleasure might excite regret when he went away, and be rewarded with the sympathy and praise of his friends, even in the presence of other minstrels. A set of verses remains, which is ascribed to him, in which he addresses the Delian women in the tone of feeling I have described. 'Farewell to you all,' he says, 'and remember me in time to come; and when any one of men on earth, a stranger from far, shall inquire of you, O maidens, who is the sweetest cf minstrels hereabout, and in whom you most delight? then make answer modestly, It is a blind man, and he lives in steep Chios.'

"The great poet remained unknown for some centuries, — that is, unknown to what we call fame. . . . At length an Athenian prince took upon him the task of gathering together the scattered fragments of a genius which had not aspired to immortality, of reducing them to writing, and of fitting them to be the text-book of ancient education. Henceforth the vagrant ballad-singer, as he might be thought, was submitted, to his surprise, to a sort of literary canonization, and was invested with the office of forming the young mind of Greece to noble thoughts and bold deeds. To be read in Homer soon became the education of a gentleman; and a rule, recognized in her free age, remained as a tradition in the times of her degradation."

Dr. Newman, it will be seen, holds by the old and natural belief that Homer was a man, not a myth. The great Teutonic hoax, which has so long glamoured the minds of the learned, seems to be somewhat losing its hold. It is a fair enough question whether the *Iliad* and the *Odyssey* are the work of the same author; also, whether certain passages in these books may not be interpolations, and whether the great creative poet may not have incorporated into his work many fragments of earlier minstrelsy. But to suppose that each of two long continuous poems, the greatest in their kind the world has seen, were the product not of one mind, but of many minds, working either with design or at haphazard, is too much for plain men to take in.

Note IV.—Page 58.

The best exposition which I have met with of the inadequacy of Phenomenalism, as a total account of the whole matter, is to be found in the late Professor Grote's *Exploratio Philosophica* (published at Cambridge in 1865). In that work he thinks over once again the fundamental problems that lie at the root of all philosophy. And though the style may be felt to be lengthy, tentative, and hesitating, yet all who care for the subjects he treats of will readily forget this for the entire freshness, honesty, and originality of the thinking. His book reads as though you overheard a real thinker thinking aloud. And much of what may be regarded as defect of style may be put down to the entire candor and thoroughness of the writer, caring far more for what he has to say, than for the manner in which he says it.

The following are some of the contrasts he draws between the phenomenal and the philosophical point of view: —

"The phenomenal verb is 'Is' in the sense of 'exist,' with immediate applications of it to certain objects of our thought itself, the nature of the existence, the grounds of our supposition of it, not entering into consideration. The verb of philosophy, or when our point of departure is consciousness or our own personality, is one which has scarcely existence in popular language: we might consider it to be 'feel' used neutrally, or 'feel ourselves' (the Greek ἔχω) with an adverb. In this consciousness, in the philosopher's point of view, is the root of all certainty or knowledge. The problem of philosophy is the finding the relation between existence and this. . . .

"The phenomenal assumption is that the world of reality exists quite independently of being known by any knowing beings in it, just the same as it would exist if there were no knowledge or feeling in any members of it. The Berkeleian idealism is little more than the easy demonstration that this view, from a philosophical standing point, is untenable;

that the notion of existence, as distinguished from perceivedness, is, nakedly and rudely stated, as abhorrent to the philosopher as that of perceivingness and will, in any part of the matter the laws of which he is seeking, is to the phenomenalist.

"I think the best way of our conceiving this phenomenalist spirit, carefully avoiding, in our *intellectual* conception of it, any moral approbation or disapprobation of it, is to conceive what exists existing without being known, — without any mind, or anything like mind, having originated it or having been concerned with its origination or arrangement, so that when we find in it anything which we should describe as order or form, or composition, it is not that kind of order, or anything like it, which we mean when we speak of putting together anything ourselves with a meaning and a reason. The phenomenalist maxim must be to put nothing (mentally) in the universe beyond what we find there ; and what we find there phenomenally is that, and nothing more, which communicates with the various natural elements, nervous matter, . . . of which our bodies are composed. We really, phenomenally, have no right to speak of order, arrangement, composition, . . . in the universe, all which are ideas belonging to our own consciousness of active and constructive powers. The great rule of phenomenalism is to be sure that we do not do that which we always naturally *do* do, humanize the universe, recognize intelligence in it, have any preliminary faith, persuasion, suppositions about it, find ourselves, if I may so speak, at all at home in it, think it has any concern with us." — (pp. 14, 15).

"The point of the difference is that in the former

(the phenomenalist point of view) we look upon what we can find out by physical research as ultimate fact, as far as we are concerned, and upon conformity with this as the test of truth; so that nothing is admitted as true except so far as it follows by some process of inference from this. In opposition to this, the contrasted view is to the effect, that for philosophy, for our entire judgment about things, we must go beyond this, or rather go further back than it. The ultimate fact really for us — the basis upon which all rests — being, not that things exist, but that we know them, *i. e.*, think of them as existing. The order of things in this view is not existence first, and then knowledge; but knowledge (or consciousness of self) first, involving or implying the existence of what is known, but logically at least prior to it, and conceivably more extensive than it. In the former view knowledge about things is looked upon as a possibly supervening accident to them or of them. In the latter view, their knowableness is a part, and the most important part, of their reality or essential being. In the former view, mind or consciousness is supposed to follow, desultorily and accidentally, after matter of fact. In the latter view, mind or consciousness begins with recognizing itself as a part of an entire supposed matter of fact or universe, and next as correspondent, in its subjective character, to the whole of this besides as object, while the understanding of this latter as *known*, germinates into the notion of the recognition of other mind or reason in it." — (p. 59.)

"We are really conscious of a non ego as of an ego, we are not therefore the only existence, and from this it seems to me to follow, that we have reason in considering that in evolving (by thought) order and character, or *somethingness* out of mere disorder, — objects out of prae-objectal possibility — we are not the only mind at work. As much as we feel ourselves mind, we feel ourselves one mind, and that there may be others. We know things, therefore, not only because *we* are, but because there are things that can be known; because there are things which have in them the quality or character of knowableness, *i. e.*, a counterpart or adaptedness to reason; which is, however we like to describe it, the same as a mind or reason so far insubstantiated or embodied." — (p. 58).

Note V. — Page 65.

For this view of the double aspect of all human action — at least for the form in which it is here put — I desire to own my obligation to a very thoughtful and searching criticism of Mr. Huxley's Lecture which shortly after that Lecture was published appeared in the *Spectator*. It is one of many papers which from time to time appear in that periodical, full of thought on the highest subjects, which is at once robust and reverential. Without in any measure indorsing the political views of that periodical, I may be allowed here to express my admiration of the papers to which I allude. They are exclusively on philosophical or religious subjects, or rather on that border land where philosophy and religion meet. One may not always agree with all that they contain. But no thoughtful person, whatever his own views may be, can read them without being braced in mind and spirit by their atmosphere of thought.

If I had at hand the number of the *Spectator* which contained the paper on Mr. Huxley's Lecture, I should have made some extracts from it in this place. But in default of this, I may be allowed, as it is pertinent to the subject of my second Lecture, to make the following quotation from the *Spectator* of July 30, 1870: — "The most dangerous form of unbelief at the present time is what we may call the 'scientific,' which says, when it contents itself with negatives, 'we do not find God or any of the spiritual things of which you speak in the world with which we have to do;' which goes further when it chooses to be aggressive, and says 'your theology is very much in the way of the improvement and advance of the human race, and we will put it out of the way.' To this, in either mood, all theologies are alike. . . . It is with this that the battle must be fought out, and to any one who can furnish weapons for it our deepest gratitude is due."

To furnish such weapons is a task I do not now venture to undertake. There are, however, certain fundamental questions which may be suggested for the consideration of those who are in the state of scientific unbelief above described, and who yet are candid men, open to conviction. It may be asked, Do you really hold that the world with which science deals is the whole world of existence? If there is a world of truth outside, or perhaps rather inside, of that which science is cognizant of, is no part of it to be believed till science has made it her own, and given us scientific grounds for believing it? You say that you do not find God in the world with which you have to do. Is, however, this world of yours the only world that really exists? Is it even the most important world,—important, that is, if you consider all that man is, all that history proves him to be and to need?

Or to put the same questions from another side. Are you quite sure that, with all your science, you have all the faculties necessary for apprehending all truth awake and active within you? May there not be other capacities of your being, than those scientific ones, which capacities you, in your entire absorption in science, have hitherto allowed to lie dormant? And if so, may not these be just the very capacities required to make you feel the need of God, and to enable you to find Him?

The truly scientific man reverences all facts. Is not this one worth his consideration? The verdict of all ages has pronounced, that the exclusively scientific man, he in whom the scientific side is everything, and the spiritual side, that is heart, conscience, spiritual aspiration, go for nothing, is but half a man, developed only on one side of his nature, and that not the highest side. If God is to be apprehended at all in a vital way, and not merely as an intellectual abstraction, it must be first from the spiritual side of our being, by the conscience, the spirit, the reverence that is in man, that he is mainly to be approached. This is the centre of the whole matter. From this side we must begin, however much may afterwards be added by experience and acquired knowledge.

I had got thus far in writing this note when I met with the following passage in a paper on Dr. Newman's *Grammar of Assent*, which appeared in the

Quarterly Review of last July, and is relevant to the matter on hand. "There are two ideas of the Divine Being which spring respectively from two sets of first principles, — one of which gathers around conscience, the other around a physical centre. There is the idea of Him as a moral governor and judge, expressed in the majestic language of inspiration, which proclaims the 'High and lofty one that inhabiteth eternity, whose name is Holy; keeping mercy for thousands, forgiving iniquity, transgression, and sin, and that will by no means clear the guilty.' And there is another idea of Him as the supreme mundane being, the impersonation of the causes which are at work in the development and completion of the visible world; who looks — we cannot say from heaven — with calm satisfaction upon the successful expansion of the original seed which commenced the formation of the vast material organism, — the universal spectator of the fabric of nature, the growth of art, and the progress of civilization. These two ideas of the Deity must make all the difference in the aspect in which a revelation presents itself to us; the former will recommend such a revelation as that in the Old and New Testament to us; the latter will create a whole foundation of thought in preliminary conflict with it."

This passage seems to represent truly the two fundamental tendencies of thought on this subject, which are seen abundantly exemplified in the present time. The scientific unbelief to which the *Spectator* alludes does not perhaps get so far as to assert a "Supreme Mundane Being," but it is along this line of thought that it travels, and this is what it would assert if it cared or ventured to assert anything. The contest between these two tendencies is a radical and irreconcilable one, — no compromise is possible. And I cannot imagine how any one who has once got into the purely physical way of conceiving the first origin of things can pass out of it into the moral and spiritual conception, except by a radical change in his whole mode of thought, an inward awakening which shall make him know and feel experimentally the need of a spiritual and moral Being on whom his own being can repose, as it never can on any physical centre.

Once more the old truth must be asserted that if we are to reach God at all, in any vital way, we must begin from the centre of conscience and the truths it contains, — from that in us which is highest and best, which highest and best, feeble though it be, is, we believe, the truest image we have of His real nature. This, in the religious region, is the centre of all light and heat. The moral and spiritual is primary and supreme. But it has always been felt that, starting from this centre, it is the function and duty of thought to radiate out, till it embraces and vitalizes all that is known and that exists. And now, more than ever, there is an urgent demand that thought should do this, — that the bearing of the moral on the physical order should be more closely pondered, — that, if it might be, the point should be described, at which the Supreme will touches and moves the fundamental forces which make up the physical universe. In this direction there lie whole worlds of undiscovered country, more important and interesting than any which philosophy and science have yet reclaimed. But this conquest will not be achieved by any movement of thought which begins by denying or throwing into the background those spiritual principles which are the most deeply rooted, and the most enduring, of any that are in man.

Note VI. — Page 122.

This thought, which has been often urged, and in many forms, is put very forcibly by the Rev. J. Llewelyn Davies in the preface to his book of sermons entitled *The Gospel and Modern Life.*

It has since the publication of these sermons been elaborately drawn out by Dr. Newman with his peculiar power, and forms a leading portion of the argument in his *Grammar of Assent.*

The following quotation is from Mr. Davies's preface: —

"The arguments by which Christians of the firmest faith are and have been always most powerfully moved, are not such as it is easy to lay out in controversy, or such as can be conveniently weighed and measured by logical instruments. . . . Christians are continually tempted to do what all controversy solicits them to do, namely, to argue as if their business was to establish, in the light of the understanding, certain conclusions to which every rational person must assent. But this is to put the main point, the attractive action of God Himself, out of the question. If the end of God be what we hold it to be, to bring human souls to Himself, then the means He actually employs must be living and spiritual. They are likely to be infinitely various and subtle, but they will deal principally with the conscience and the affections. God is likely — nay, is certain — to manifest Himself more and more in proportion to faith and love. Christian appeals belong naturally to a region that may be called mystical, or may be otherwise described as personal and spiritual. The experience of the inner life, rightly understood and tested, is the best evidence that can be adduced. Words which one man can say out of his heart may strongly move another man. If we will not acknowledge evidence of this kind, the evidence does not perish or lose its power, but we are simply remaining on the outside of the question.

"No Christian need be ashamed of trying to rise into the sphere of those motives, and to submit to the government of those influences which have produced all that is best in Christendom. But the truth is that no one, Christian or non-Christian, can become serious and think of what he himself lives by and for, without appealing to considerations which may incur the taunt of being personal and mystical."

Note VII. — Page 139.

"When, then, even an unlearned person thus trained, — from his own heart, from the action of his mind upon itself, from struggles with self, from an attempt to follow those impulses of his own nature which he feels to be highest and noblest, from a vivid natural perception (natural, though cherished and strengthened by prayer; natural, though unfolded and diversified by practice; natural, though of that new and second nature which God the Holy Ghost gives), from an innate, though supernatural perception of the great vision of truth which is external to him (a perception of it, not indeed in its fullness, but in glimpses, and by fits and seasons, and in its persuasive influences, and through a courageous following on after it, as a man in the dark might follow after some dim and distant light), — I say, when a person thus trained from his own heart, reads the declarations and promises of the Gospel, are we to be told that he believes in them merely because he has been bid believe in them? Do we not see that he has something in his own breast which bears a confirming testimony to their truth? He reads that the heart is 'deceitful above all things and desperately wicked,' and that he inherits an evil nature from Adam, and that he is still under its power, except so far as he has been renewed. Here is a mystery; but his own actual and too bitter experience bears witness to the truth of the declaration; he feels the mystery of iniquity within him. He reads that 'without holiness no man shall see the Lord;' and his own love of what is true and lovely and pure approves and embraces the doctrine as coming from God. He reads that God is angry at sin, and will punish the sinner, and that it is a hard matter, nay, an impossibility, for us to appease His wrath. Here, again, is a mystery; but here, too, his conscience anticipates the mystery, and convicts him; his mouth is stopped. And when he goes on to read that the Son of God has Himself come into the world in our flesh, and died upon the Cross for us, does he not, amid the awful mysteriousness of the doctrine, find those words fulfilled in him which that gracious Saviour uttered: 'And I, if I be lifted up from the earth, will draw all men unto me?' He cannot choose but believe in Him. He says, 'O

Lord, Thou art stronger than I, and hast prevailed.'" — Dr. Newman's *Parochial and Plain Sermons* (Ed. 1868), vol. viii. pp. 117–119.

NOTE VIII. — Page 165.

"WE are not to be impatient of mystery — which encompasses us on all sides. Our God gives us light, and we are to walk in it and rejoice in it; but this light seems to have ever beyond it a region of darkness. The light is not on that account less truly light, and to be trusted in as light. To permit darkness to bring light into question — to feel sure of nothing because we cannot know all things — is in truth to do violence to the constitution of our being, to which if we are faithful, we shall know light to be really light, whatever outer circle of darkness may make itself felt by us. Let us thankfully rejoice in the light and reverently submit to the darkness. And let us welcome that gradual widening of the region of light, of which we have experience, the retiring of the circle of encompassing darkness. How far remaining darkness may yet give place to light now or hereafter in the endless eternity before us we know not. In the mean time we honor the light by obeying it, and in so doing honor God, while we honor Him also by a right aspect of our minds towards the darkness, accepting our limits in the faith of the wise love which appoints them. For if we are giving God glory in what He gives us to know, it will not be difficult to give Him the further glory of being peaceful and at rest concerning the darkness which remains; not doubting that what we know not must be in harmony with what we know; and would be seen by us to be so, if God saw it good that the remaining darkness should altogether pass away: if indeed it is possible in the nature of things that it should pass away. For we can believe that much is embraced in the divine consciousness and in the relation of the creature to God, which it may be incompatible with creature limits that we should know. Yet on the other hand that is a large word, 'Then shall we know even as we also are known.'" — *Christ the Bread of Life,* by John M'Leod Campbell, D. D. (Second Edition), pp. 157, 158.

www.ingramcontent.com/pod-product-compliance
Lightning Source LLC
LaVergne TN
LVHW011219110826
845150LV00006B/1471